American Idol

Official Behind-the-Scenes Fan Book

SEASON 4

Jason R. Rich

Prima Games
A Division of Random House, Inc.
3000 Lava Ridge Court, Suite 100
Roseville, CA 95661
1-800-733-3000
primagames.com

Credits

Author: Jason R. Rich

Product Manager: Jill Hinckley

Editor: Rebecca Chastain

Designers: Jamie A. Knight
Marc Riegel
Rick Wong

Photographer: Lisa Stahl Sullivan

FremantleMedia:

Cecile Frot-Coutaz

Simon Spalding

Olivier Gers

David Luner

Michael Jaffa

James Ngo

Rebecca Morris

Emma Gordon

Toby Prosser

American Idol Productions:

Simon Fuller

Nigel Lythgoe

Ken Warwick

Bruce Gowers

Wylleen May

Charles Boyd

James Breen

Patrick M. Lynn

Simon Lythgoe

Michelle Baker

Megan Michaels

Brian Robinson

Jessica Kelly

Acknowledgments

Allow me to thank Simon Lythgoe, Patrick Lynn, Megan Michaels, Wylleen May, Michelle Baker, Olivier Gers, David Luner, James Ngo, Jason Turner, Michele Welch, Wendy Myo-Tsang, Andy Felsher, Megan Wallace, Michael Jaffa, Charles Boyd, James Breen, Lisl Wright, Norm Betts, Sophia Reichenbach, Debra Byrd, Michael Orland, Susan Slamer, Rickey Minor, John Beasley, Dorian Holly, Miles Siggins, Dean Banowetz, Carrie Ann Inaba, Mandy Moore, and Michael Boschetti for their support.

A special thanks to photographer extraordinaire Lisa Sullivan.

Finally, thanks to everyone at Prima/Random House, including Debra, Julie, Jill, Rebecca, Andy, Erica, and Louisa for making this book a reality and for allowing me to work on such an amazing project!

—Jason

The Prima Games logo is a registered trademark of Random House, Inc., registered in the United States and other countries. Primagames.com is a registered trademark of Random House, Inc., registered in the United States.

© 2005 by Prima Games. All rights reserved. No part of this book may be reproduced or transmitted in any form or by any means, electronic or mechanical, including photocopying, recording, or by any information storage or retrieval system without written permission from Prima Games. Prima Games is a division of Random House, Inc.

American Idol is a trademark of 19 TV Limited and FremantleMedia North America, Inc. Based on the television program 'American Idol' produced by FremantleMedia North America, Inc. and 19 TV Limited. Licensed by FremantleMedia Licensing Worldwide. www.fremantlemedia.com. ©2005 FremantleMedia North America, Inc. All Rights Reserved.

All products and characters mentioned in this book are trademarks of their respective companies.

Important:
Prima Games has made every effort to determine that the information contained in this book is accurate. However, the publisher makes no warranty, either expressed or implied, as to the accuracy, effectiveness, or completeness of the material in this book; nor does the publisher assume liability for damages, either incidental or consequential, that may result from using the information in this book.

ISBN: 0-7615-4946-3
Library of Congress Catalog Card Number: 2005920950
Printed in the United States of America

05 06 07 08 LL 10 9 8 7 6 5 4 3 2 1

Contents

What started out as a televised talent competition in the United Kingdom, called *Pop Idol*, has grown into a worldwide phenomenon that has launched the mega-successful careers of multiple recording artists throughout the world.

The Worldwide Phenomenon Continues

In January 2005, a record number of viewers tuned in to The Fox Television Network for the season premier of *American Idol* Season 4, immediately making it the #1 most watched show on TV with 33.5 million viewers! For Season 4, the producers added a few twists to make the competition even more exciting, not just for the participants, but for the viewers as well.

Of course, Simon Cowell continued to offer his often harsh criticisms, while viewers voted for their favorite contestants. This season, however, the age limit for participants changed and the process for narrowing down the pool of contestants was different. More than 100,000 people auditioned for *American Idol* 4, yet after several rounds of grueling auditions, the number of contestants was ultimately reduced to just 24 hopefuls.

From there, it became a "guys-versus-girls" competition, as additional contestants were voted off the show by America's TV viewers. By mid-March 2005, America got its first peek at the Top 12 contestants and began deciding whom their next American Idol would ultimately be.

Following in the incredibly successful footsteps of Kelly Clarkson (Season 1 winner),

Ruben Studdard (Season 2 winner), Clay Aiken (Season 2 runner-up), Fantasia Barrino (Season 3 winner), and Diana DeGarmo (Season 3 runner-up), a brand-new pop star was in the making as the *American Idol* 4 season got underway.

It's A Worldwide Phenomenon

In addition to *American Idol*, there are currently 30 versions of the show in production throughout the world. In almost every country where a version of *Idol* airs, it's typically the #1-rated television show. Plus, television viewers worldwide also get to watch the *American Idol* competition unfold.

So, if you happen to be vacationing in Australia, for example, chances are you'll be able to catch *Australian Idol* as well as *American Idol*. Other versions of the show include *Pop Idol* (in the United Kingdom), *Canadian Idol*, Greece's *Super Idol*, *Singapore Idol*, *South Africa Idol*, and Germany's *Deutschland Sucht Den Superstar*.

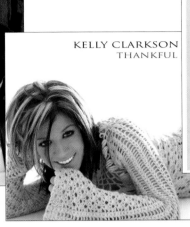
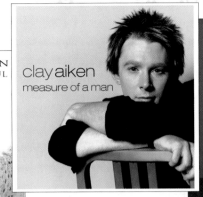
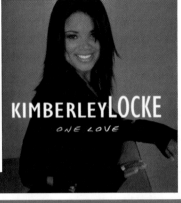

The #1 hits keep coming from past *American Idol* winners and runners-up.

It's More Than Just a TV Show

Not only has *American Idol* launched the careers of several popular recording artists, it's also been directly responsible for helping those artists sell millions of CDs and get airplay on radio stations across the country. Clay Aiken, for example, has embarked on several sold-out tours, hosted his own network television special, recorded several #1 hit songs, written a bestselling book, launched his own charitable foundation (the Bubel/Aiken Foundation), and continues to release new CDs and videos for his fans.

After each *American Idol* season, fans of the show get to see the Top 10 contestants perform live as the *American Idol Live!* tour makes its way across America. Meanwhile, for those who can't get enough of this mega-hit TV show, there are dozens of officially licensed *American Idol* products, like Barbie dolls, trading cards, a magazine, a cell phone, clothing, a karaoke machine, jewelry, and, of course, the book you're reading right now. By the way, if you want to reminisce about Season 3, be sure to pick up your copy of *American Idol Season 3: All Access* wherever books are sold!

What Makes *American Idol* So Special?

There are many reasons why *American Idol* continues to be the most popular televised talent competition in the country. Some viewers tune in simply to watch the performances. Each season, we get to know a handful of new contestants, watch them perform, and see them transform into pop superstars.

And of course, there are the judges. Simon Cowell, Randy Jackson, and Paula Abdul continue to offer witty and often harsh criticisms of each performance, which often makes for exciting viewing. What will Simon say next? How will he manage to insult one of the contestants? To find out, you need to watch the show!

American Idol also gets television viewers directly involved by allowing them to vote for their favorite contestants each and every week. Ultimately, it's America that chooses their next American Idol. Each week, over 33.5 million votes are cast as fans call in their support for the contestant they want to win.

With his always-perfect hair and ultra-trendy wardrobe, host Ryan Seacrest offers his unique brand of humor as he tries to keep the judges in line, encourages the contestants, and builds up the suspense for viewers at home.

Simon Cowell, Randy Jackson, and Paula Abdul are *American Idol*'s famous judges.

Another element of *American Idol* that keeps viewers glued to their television sets is the show's evolution over the season. The first few episodes of the season are pretaped recaps of the auditions. Here, we get to see some of the best (and absolute worst) people who auditioned for the show. Then, as the contestant pool shrinks, viewers watch the Hollywood audition phase, where the remaining finalists are put through a series of challenges.

With just 24 contestants remaining in the competition, the live competition and results shows start airing from the *American Idol* set. Viewers watch each performer as he or she deals with the stress of singing live on national television in front of the judges, a studio audience, and millions of critical viewers watching at home. One mistake and a contestant could quickly be voted off the show.

For the final 11 weeks of the competition, the remaining contestants perform every Tuesday night on the famous *American Idol* stage. Then, on Wednesday nights, it's revealed which unlucky person voters have eliminated from the show that week.

In May, when only two finalists remain, the show really gets exciting! From the Kodak Theater in Hollywood, California, the two-night season finale of *American Idol* airs live. This time, a theater audience made up of several thousand screaming fans and celebrities, plus an incredibly large television audience, all anxiously wait for Ryan Seacrest to reveal the winner.

During the *American Idol* 3 season finale, Ryan announced Fantasia had won!

American Idol offers entertaining performances, laughs, suspense, drama, excitement, and plenty of tears as the contestants and television viewers alike experience the emotional rollercoaster that makes this show what it is.

What keeps *American Idol* so popular is the amazingly talented team of producers and crew members who work behind the scenes to get this show on the air. Under the leadership of executive producers Simon Fuller, Nigel Lythgoe, Ken Warwick, and Cecile Frot-Coutaz, the crew working on *American Idol* is truly the best in the business!

American Idol is a television phenomenon that's unlike any other. It's a unique show that continues to break ratings records as it entertains millions of television viewers throughout the world.

And the Next American Idol Winner Is...

You're about to go behind the scenes of *American Idol* and discover contestant information that you didn't see on television! You'll read exclusive interviews with *American Idol* 4's Top 12 contestants, see hundreds of never-before-seen photos, and discover exactly what each finalist experienced throughout the *American Idol* 4 season. You'll witness the transformations of a dozen talented people as they become some of the most popular performers in America.

Get ready to experience a true behind-the-scenes look at *American Idol* Season 4!

Meet *American Idol* Season 4's Top 12 contestants!

Season three of *American Idol* ended with record ratings. Over 50 million people watched as Fantasia beat out Diana to become the third winner of television's most popular talent competition.

The American Idol 4 Auditions: Here We Go Again!

As summer 2004 rolled around, it was time for the judges, a team of producers, and *American Idol*'s camera crews to set off on another cross-country journey in search of a new American Idol for season four. This time, anyone between the ages of 16 and 28 was allowed to audition. In previous years, the cut-off age was 25.

For *American Idol* 4, auditions were held in St. Louis, Missouri; Las Vegas, Nevada; San Francisco, California; Washington, DC; New Orleans, Louisiana; Cleveland, Ohio; and Orlando, Florida. More than 100,000 people (that's 30,000 more people than last year) showed up for their chance to perform for the judges.

In Orlando (at the Orleans Arena) and in the six other cities, anywhere from 10,000 to 20,000 singers auditioned for their chance at superstardom.

Most people brought sleeping bags, books, magazines, guitars, Game Boys, board games, and other activities to help them pass the time as they camped out for between one and three days.

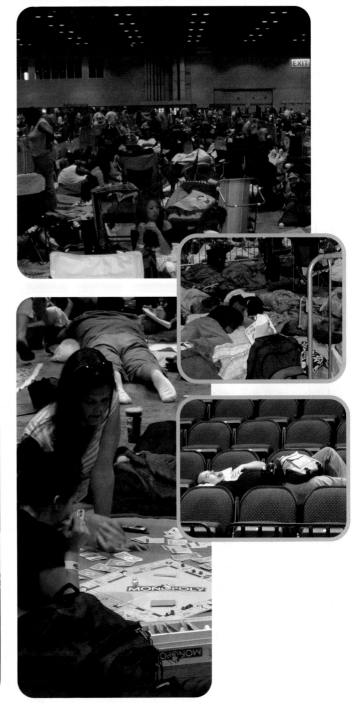

Contestants Must Impress the American Idol Team

Before contestants got a chance to perform for the judges, they first needed to get past two rounds of preliminary judging.

After camping out, then standing in long lines for countless hours, each hopeful had only approximately 30 seconds to sing part of any song for one of the show's producers. Those who didn't make the cut were quickly sent home, while those relative few who showed signs of talent moved on to the next phase of the auditions.

For the lucky and talented bunch who got through the first round of auditions, the next stop was to perform one or two songs for Nigel Lythgoe and Ken Warwick, *American Idol*'s executive producers. Only those who managed to impress Nigel and Ken got a chance to step in front of Simon, Paula, and Randy.

In each city, the three judges, sometimes accompanied by a guest judge, like Gene Simmons, LL Cool J, or Brandy, met with several hundreds contestants who made it through the first two rounds of auditions.

The goal here was to earn a "Golden Ticket" from the judges—an invitation to Hollywood to participate in round two of the competition. Out of the more than 100,000 people who auditioned, only about 300 ultimately received a "Golden Ticket."

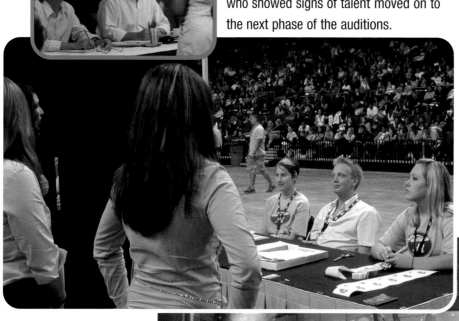

The Hollywood Auditions

In early-November, 2004, the 300 contestants who earned "Golden Tickets" were flown to Hollywood. For almost a week, they participated in a series of stressful and extremely challenging auditions in front of the three judges.

By the end of the Hollywood auditions week, only 48 contestants remained in the *American Idol* 4 competition. One of these people would ultimately become the next *American Idol*!

This round of auditions took place at the historic Orpheum Theater in downtown Los Angeles.

During this hectic week, each contestant had to perform solo for the judges. The entire time, the TV cameras were rolling! Within 24 hours after everyone arrived in Hollywood, the judges cut the contestant pool from 300 to just 150.

At one point, the judges divided the remaining contestants into groups of three. In less than 12 hours, they needed to get to know each other, learn a new song, develop choreography, then perform together as if they were a new pop trio.

Halfway through the Hollywood auditions, the remaining 75 contestants posed for a photo in the Orpheum Theater with Ryan Seacrest.

Each contestant had several opportunities to perform solo in front of the judges. Sometimes they had musical accompaniment, while other times they had to sing a cappella (without music).

Next Stop: Pasadena

Those who survived the Hollywood auditions had to wait until early January to discover if they'd make the final cut and earn a spot in the Top 24. During this time, the judges carefully reviewed all the audition tapes, then from the Top 48, they selected 12 guys and 12 girls who would make up this season's Top 24.

After the decisions were made, the Top 48 contestants were flown to Pasadena, California to learn their fate.

At this point in the *American Idol* competition, the rules changed. Instead of the judges' opinions, it was America's votes that cut the group from the Top 24 to the Top 12. During this phase of *American Idol* 4, it was an entertaining guys-versus-girls competition, with live shows airing three times per week on FOX.

Watch out William Hung! You've got competition!

This Season, the Bad Got Worse!

Mary Roach

Age: 18

Hometown: Manassas, VA

Audition City: Washington, DC

If one person this season gave William Hung a run for his money, it was Mary Roach. Not only was this cosmetology student convinced she could sing, but the voices she hears in her head totally agreed with her. When she sang Carol King's "I Feel The Earth Move," the judges seemed to want to quickly move out of the room.

When asked how she thought she did, Mary's response was, "Not too shabby!" Needless to say, Simon didn't agree. He exclaimed, "Honestly, one of the worst I've ever heard in my life…What made you audition for this competition? Mary, you can't sing…You have one of the weirdest voices I've heard in my life." Maybe Mary should stick to cosmetology school.

Leandra Jackson

Age: 20

Hometown: Cleveland, OH

Audition City: Washington, DC

Major League Baseball and other professional sporting events kick off games with someone singing the national anthem, "The Star-Spangled Banner," so why shouldn't *American Idol*? Leandra Jackson offered her unique rendition of our country's most patriotic song. But, instead of rising to pay respect to our fine country, perhaps the audience should have called Immigration to have this *American Idol* hopeful deported.

She put a lot of emotion behind her performance, and if the judges had been basing their picks on that, Leandra would have been off to Hollywood. Unfortunately, this is a vocal competition.

Mellissa Considine

Age: 20

Hometown: Tom's River, NJ

Audition City: Washington, DC

Before Melissa auditioned, she told host Ryan Seacrest that she likes to stand out through her style and overall appearance. Simon, however, didn't like her look. Moreover, he didn't like Melissa's voice either. As she walked into the audition room, Simon said, "You look like you've been dragged through a bush. You're covered in scratches." He also made a comment about her outfit and her excessive use of fashion accessories.

Minutes later, Melissa absolutely butchered "America the Beautiful" during her audition. "I never thought I'd say this, but you actually dress better than you sing. That was unbelievable….There's not a song in the world you could sing in tune. You have an absolutely horrible singing voice," said Simon.

What did Melissa learn from her experience? You may not need a lot of money to look nice, but you do need some taste and fashion sense. As for her singing, let's just say Fantasia, Ruben, and Kelly have absolutely nothing to worry about.

Okay folks, in case you haven't figured it out by now, *American Idol* is a *talent* competition that looks for the next pop superstar. Considering that a record number of fans watched the show during the past three seasons, you'd think people would catch on to the fact that if they can't sing and have no talent, they have no business whatsoever attending the auditions.

Well, that didn't stop thousands of untalented people from showing up in one or more of the AI4 audition cities for their chance to sing for the judges and the TV cameras. As in previous years, there were definitely a handful of outrageous, funny, and really awful singers that nobody could forget.

Mandy, Erin, & Melissa Maynard

Age: 18

Hometown: Omaha, NE

Audition City: St. Louis, MO

It seems that identical triplets Mandy, Erin, and Melissa didn't get the memo that *American Idol* was searching for a *solo* pop artist. The trio decided to show up to the auditions and perform together. That was mistake number one.

Their second big problem was that the judges didn't think they had talent. Mandy and Melissa agreed that Erin is the most talented of the three. After less than ten seconds of singing, Simon said, "You're like three overweight Jessica Simpsons...That's the truth. I can't put you through as a group."

After dismissing Mandy and Melissa, Randy wanted to put Erin through to Hollywood, but both Simon and Paula sent all three girls home. Like Jessica, maybe the triplets should star in their own reality TV series. Hey MTV, we've got a show idea for you!

Bobby Barfoot

Age: 26

Hometown: Layette Ville, NC

Audition City: New Orleans, LA

Okay, Bobby might have dressed a little strangely. He also demonstrated on national television that he couldn't sing, but he could yodel like an absolute pro. This *American Idol* mega-fan proved one thing, however: he has great taste in reading material. Just before his audition, Bobby proudly showed off his copy of *American Idol Season 3: All Access*, last season's official *American Idol* book! As for his audition, here's how Simon described it. "It was a cross between a rodeo and *La Cage Au Folles*." At least this season, Bobby can read about himself when he buys the official *American Idol* book.

Jessica Pontius

Age: 16

Hometown: Indianapolis, IN

Audition City: St. Louis, MO

Dressed in a lovely pink outfit, Jessica performed "Somewhere over the Rainbow" for the judges. As soon as she opened her mouth, however, Toto called the ASPCA to complain about animal abuse, while the judges laughed and sent Jessica following the yellow brick road back home.

"That was honestly, excruciatingly awful...Honestly awful," said Simon. Randy added, "Singing isn't your thing." It was Paula, however, who suggested that Jessica pursue work as a voice-over actress for cartoons, perhaps giving the voice to an animated rat. Instead of responding, Jessica simply walked out of the audition room.

Leroy Wells

Age: 22

Hometown: Grand Bay, AL

Audition City: New Orleans, LA

Can you dig it? No really, can you dig it? Leroy Wells certainly could! "Can you dig it?" was the only intelligible phrase that came out of his mouth during his entire audition. Leroy clearly wanted to be on television and was willing to act like an absolute fool to achieve his objective.

"You're energetic and fun, but this isn't the right competition for you," said Paula. After sitting through Leroy's audition, Simon, Paul, Randy, and guest judge Gene Simmons, learned that they, too, could dig it.

Sundeep Achreja

Age: 28

Hometown: Metairie, LA

Audition City: New Orleans, LA

He was immaculately dressed for his audition. Plus, as a successful accountant, Sundeep is clearly highly intelligent. So, what made him think he should audition for *American Idol*? This guy certainly wasn't *American Idol* material, but if the show's producers decide to launch an *American Idol* basketball team, thanks to his height, you can bet Sundeep will be the first person they'll call.

During his audition, Sundeep sang his own rendition of "Eye of the Tiger." Not only was he off-key throughout the entire song, he demonstrated absolutely no emotion or personality. All Paula could say was, "Do you ever watch the show?" At least Sundeep was proud of himself for not forgetting any lyrics.

Jeffrey "J.C." Gray

Age: 24
Hometown: Las Vegas, NV
Audition City: Las Vegas, NV

Jeffrey Gray claims to be one of Neil Diamond's biggest fans. He was deaf as a child, he currently works as a fast food cook, and he has the widest eyes ever to be seen on television. With his hair slicked back, Jeffrey belted out his own idol's biggest hit, "America."

Throughout his performance, Jeffrey kept making stabbing motions with his right arm, as if he were trying to murder the song. What he didn't realize was that his voice was already butchering the melody.

Oddly enough, Jeffrey wasn't a hit with the judges. "That was slightly disturbing," said Simon after the audition. Well, at least Jeffrey took a stab at achieving his dream to be a pop star. Based on his look and mannerisms, what he'd be better suited to audition for is a guest starring role as a serial killer on a crime drama.

Matthew Falber

Age: 21
Hometown: Casper, WY
Audition City: Las Vegas, NV

Singers are supposed to convey emotion and feel their lyrics as they perform a song. Matthew took that concept a step further when he reenacted several of the character's voices from *The Lion King* while he performed "I Just Can't Wait to be King" during his audition. He even used his voice to create some of the instrumentals.

There's already a King of Pop, and while Matthew could hold a tune (sort of), the judges didn't want him roaring on the *American Idol* set, so they sent him back to Pride Rock. "I think you're an entertainer…Be excited that you made it this far and come back next season," said Paula. Perhaps next season, Matthew will perform selected scenes from Disney's *Aladdin* or even *The Little Mermaid*.

Sarah Sue Kelly

Age: 18
Hometown: Hillsdale, IN
Audition City: Cleveland, OH

If *American Idol*'s winner was selected based solely on personality, Sarah Sue would win the competition hands down. This delightful young girl was thrilled to take a break from her karaoke business and audition for the judges. One of her first mistakes, however, was choosing a song from a Broadway show, instead of a pop song.

"If I'm being honest, it's the way you look that's putting us off…. You don't have to be a Barbie, but I am giving you a reality check, Sarah. I think you have a nice voice. This is a business where people will judge you on the way you look. I'm not saying that I'm like that [yeah, right!], but people are," said Simon.

Jennifer Page

Age: 20
Hometown: Brecksville, OH
Audition City: Cleveland, OH

Proving that you don't have to sing a note to make it onto *American Idol* (at least during the audition episodes), Jennifer threw on some white face paint and performed an Aerosmith song as a mime. You know mimes—clown-like people who don't talk, or in this case, sing. Jennifer claimed to be a "voice" for oppressed mimes everywhere.

"That was one of the best we've heard in the competition," said Simon with a smile. Randy added, "Her pitch was spot on." Well, Jennifer might have fallen flat on her face (literally), but she did offer the judges an entertaining break from hearing some truly dreadful performers.

Season 4: It's A Whole New Competition

To make things exciting, the producers added a few surprise twists this season. Unlike last season, Season 4 had no wild card show and no semi-final group rounds. Instead, during this year's semi-final rounds, the Top 12 guys went head-to-head against the Top 12 girls, until only a dozen finalists remained.

While in Pasadena, the Top 24 took part in their first official photo shoot. Aloha Mischeaux had a blast posing for the camera and letting her personality shine.

Anthony Fedorov called home to share the good news with his family. He made it into the Top 24! Could this hottie become the next *American Idol*?

Bo Bice was a bit nervous to have the make-up artist and hairstylist get him ready for his first photo shoot in Pasadena.

Meet American Idol 4's Top 24: The Guys

Harold "Bo" Bice
Age: 28
Hometown: Atlanta, GA

David Brown
Age: 20
Hometown: New Orleans, LA

Anthony Fedorov
Age: 19
Hometown: New York, NY

Judd Harris
Age: 27
Hometown: New York, NY

Constantine Maroulis
Age: 28
Hometown: New York, NY

Joseph "Joe" Murena, Jr.
Age: 26
Hometown: Long Island, NY

Anwar Robinson
Age: 25
Hometown: Newark, NJ

Scott Savol
Age: 28
Hometown: Shaker Heights, OH

Osborne "Nikko" E. Smith II
Age: 22
Hometown: St. Louis, MO

Travis Tucker
Age: 21
Hometown: Manassas, VA

Mario Vazquez
Age: 27
Hometown: Bronx, NY

Jared Yates
Age: 18
Hometown: Danville, IL

Meet American Idol 4's Top 24: *The Girls*

Amanda Avila
Age: 23
Hometown: Las Vegas, NV

Celena Batchelor
Age: 28
Hometown: Ft. Worth, TX

Lindsey Cardinale
Age: 19
Hometown: New Orleans, LA

Janay Castine
Age: 17
Hometown: Atlanta, GA

Mikalah Gordon
Age: 16
Hometown: Las Vegas, NV

Melinda Lira
Age: 19
Hometown: Hanford, CA

Sarah Mather
Age: 22
Hometown: Wilmington, NC

Aloha Mischeaux
Age: 19
Hometown: St. Louis, MO

Jessica Sierra
Age: 19
Hometown: Tampa, FL

Vonzell Solomon
Age: 20
Hometown: Ft. Myers, FL

Nadia Turner
Age: 27
Hometown: Miami, FL

Carrie Underwood
Age: 21
Hometown: Chocotah, OK

America Voted: The Top 12

For three weeks in a row, starting in mid-February, 2005, the guys performed on Monday nights, followed by the girls performing on Tuesdays. During each week's Wednesday night results show, two guys and two girls (the contestants with the fewest votes) were cut from the competition.

By mid-March 2005, millions of votes had already been cast and the Top 12 contestants—six guys and six girls—were selected. From this point on, every Tuesday night the remaining contestants performed and America cast their votes. Then, during the Wednesday night results show, Ryan revealed who was eliminated.

As we'll discover here, this part of *American Idol* Season 4 was an extremely hectic 12 weeks for the contestants. You're about to go behind the scenes to see exactly what happened

as they prepared for each week's shows and dealt with all the stress, challenges, and excitement that comes with being a finalist on the most watched television show in America.

You'll share their tears, their laughs, their fears, their stress, and their heartbreak, as one by one the Top 12 contestants were voted off the show, despite their best efforts and amazing talent. You'll also meet many of the people who worked behind the scenes to transform the Top 12 finalists from everyday people into pop superstars.

During each week of the competition, the contestants worked 12- to 18-hour days, seven days per week, with literally no time off. There were countless hours of rehearsals with the show's vocal coaches and associate music directors (Debra Byrd, Michael Orland, Dorian

Holly, and John Beasley), as they prepared for their performances.

That was only the beginning, however. A whole team of fashion stylists, hairstyles, choreographers, dozens of producers, camera crews, and countless other show biz professionals worked with each of the contestants, making demands on them throughout each week.

Ultimately, on May 25, 2005, just one person—the next *American Idol*—will be crowned during the show's exciting two-hour season finale. Season 1 made Kelly Clarkson a household name. As Season 2 ended, both Ruben Studdard and Clay Aiken reached superstar status. Last season, it was Fantasia who took America by storm.

Who will be the next *American Idol*? You're about to get a sneak peak at parts of *American Idol* you never saw on television!

You've heard the outrageous rumors. Now, discard the gossip and discover the true answers to some of the most frequently asked questions about *American Idol*! You're about to get the inside scoop from the show's executive producer and other members of the production team.

American Idol Exposed:
Answers to the Top 10 Most Frequently Asked Questions

Nigel Lythgoe is one of *American Idol*'s executive producers. He and Ken Warwick are totally in charge!

Q: Is the voting on *American Idol* rigged?

A: "Absolutely not! The telephone voting is managed by Cingular/AT&T. The information is then sent to an outside company, called Telescope, which monitors the voting process and ultimately informs us of the results. The producers and FOX Television have absolutely nothing to do with the voting or how the votes are calculated. We have an independent agency overseeing all aspects of the voting process. I learn the results Wednesday morning, between midnight and 2:00 AM. Once the results are calculated, only Ken Warwick and I, Standards and Practices at FOX, and our Senior Vice President of Legal and Business Affairs, Michael Jaffa,

know the results before they're announced on television. We give Ryan Seacrest, the show's director, the audio engineer, and the band the results just moments before each Wednesday night's results show begins," explained Nigel.

Q: Why did Top 12 finalist Mario Vasquez leave the show so suddenly?

A: "Mario came to see Ken and me and discussed with us his personal reasons for wanting to leave the show. During those discussions, we promised Mario we would never discuss what those personal reasons are with anyone else, which is why I am not going to discuss them now. It was entirely Mario's decision to leave *American Idol*. Be assured that absolutely none of the rumors that have been circulating on the Internet, for example, are true. It's all based on speculation, gossip, and stupidity," said Nigel.

Simon and Paula often have different opinions about performances.

Q: Do judges Simon Cowell and Paula Abdul argue all the time off the set of *American Idol*?

A: "Paula and Simon are like an old married couple who love each other, but who bicker all the time," stated Nigel. "When they agree, they get along very, very well. They're both very passionate people with strong opinions. Sparks fly between them. As the show's producer, I'm here to make a television show. I enjoy the arguments between them. I try to find ways to make them clash."

Q: Where do the Top 12 finalists live during the *American Idol* season?

A: Once again, Nigel gave us the details. "During Season 4, for as long as they remain on the show, the Top 12 finalists live in an apartment complex that's located not too far from the *American Idol* studios. Each finalist has at least one roommate or shares an apartment. Unlike the *American Idol* mansion where we've housed past seasons' contestants, this arrangement gives the finalists more privacy and space. They also get their laundry done, housekeeping services once per week, and a private chef several nights per week. They work very hard every day. We want the finalists to be comfortable during what little private time they have."

Q: What happens to a contestant after they're voted off the show?

A: "Within moments after the results show ends, they're brought upstairs and debriefed by our publicist and the producers. They're also encouraged to speak with our in-house psychologist if they wish to. Wednesday night, we host a farewell dinner for the finalist voted off the show, which all of the remaining contestants, a few of the producers, and some of the finalist's friends and family members can attend. On Thursday morning, starting at about 5:00 AM, the person voted off the show does several hours worth of live radio and television interviews. After that, they return home," said Nigel.

Q: Do the finalists have a curfew when they have to be back home to their apartment every night?

A: "On the night before a live show, all of the finalists have to be back at their apartment by 10:00 PM. On other nights, their curfew is 11:00 PM, regardless of how old the finalist is," said Patrick Lynn, *American Idol*'s coordinating producer.

Q: Do the Top 12 finalists need to buy and select their own outfits to wear on the show?

A: Miles Siggins, *American Idol*'s fashion consultant, explained that each week, the finalists are given a budget to go shopping for a wardrobe to wear on Tuesday and Wednesday nights' shows. While Miles or his assistant goes shopping with each finalist individually, they're free to wear their own clothing, also.

Q: How do you get tickets to be in the *American Idol* studio audience?

A: There are several ways to get tickets for *American Idol* if you'll be visiting Los Angeles and want to be an audience member. First, you can go to the idolonfox.com website; click on "Show Info." You can also call On Camera Audiences at (818) 295-2700 to request free tickets. Another alternative is to show up at CBS Television Center early in the morning on a show day and stand in line in hopes of scoring an available seat. This last method, however, doesn't guarantee admission.

Q: How come after some of the performances, the judges say the singer was "pitchy," but the singer sounded perfectly fine on television?

A: "I wish I knew why the judges refer to some performances as 'pitchy,' even when they're not," explained Debra Byrd, one of *American Idol*'s two vocal coaches. "My own theory is that where the judges are sitting, there's so much audience noise, it's sometimes hard for them to hear. There are many speakers throughout where the audience sits. Sometimes, it's just too loud for the judges to truly hear the quality of the vocals. I think people should vote based on what they personally hear on television and how a contestant's performance strikes them. If something about a performance touches you, that person deserves your vote. There is absolutely no lip-syncing on this show. Everything you hear out of the contestants' mouths is totally live."

Q: If someone wants to audition for Season 5 of *American Idol*, where can they get the information about audition cities, dates, times, and rules?

A: Expect the producers and judges to visit a handful of cities during the summer of 2005. For specific dates, locations, and details, visit the idolonfox.com website. Make sure you read all the rules posted on the Web site and show up to the auditions totally prepared. If you'll be "camping out" for a day or more, bring a sleeping bag, pillow, and stuff to do. Most importantly, know your music and be able to sing it perfectly.

As an expert fashion consultant, each week Miles goes shopping with the finalists when they need outfits to wear on the show.

Famous Faces

While some people are literally addicted to *American Idol* because of the amazingly talented singers who perform each week on the show, what many viewers really love is when Simon Cowell offers his brutally honest and often harsh criticism of each performance. Contestants have been known to leave the stage in tears after hearing what Simon had to say about them.

Of course, every episode of *American Idol* showcases the ongoing bickering between Simon and Paula Abdul, the insults that are traded between host Ryan Seacrest and the judges, and the ever-present challenge of having to decode what Randy Jackson says, since he usually uses the word "dawg" at least once in every sentence.

So, while the contestants provide the musical entertainment, it's often the show's host and judges who make *American Idol* truly worth watching.

If you're wondering how Simon Cowell, Paula Abdul, and Randy Jackson were selected to be the judges for *American Idol*, the answer is easy. As you're about to discover, each of the three judges is literally an expert in their field. Simon Cowell is an extremely successful record label executive, Randy Jackson is an equally successful music producer, and Paula Abdul is a former chart-topping recording artist.

Because each judge has their own unique thoughts and criticisms, there's often disagreement among the trio. It's the responsibility of Ryan, as the show's host, to ensure that everything runs smoothly during each live *American Idol* broadcast.

Ryan Seacrest

Ryan checks out last year's official *American Idol* book, *American Idol Season 3: All Access* (Prima/Random House).

American Idol's host, Ryan Seacrest, has become one of the most recognizable faces on TV and is now among the most familiar voices you'll hear on the radio. In addition to hosting *American Idol* for all four exciting seasons, he's also the morning host and executive producer of *On-Air with Ryan Seacrest*, which airs weekdays on KIIS-FM (one of the most popular radio stations in Los Angeles).

If you don't live in the Los Angeles area, you can also catch Ryan hosting *American Top 40*, which airs on radio stations each week across America. This show alone attracts a weekly audience of more than 3.1 million dedicated listeners.

One thing you can count on when you see Ryan on TV is that he'll look good. He's become the poster boy for "metrosexuals" everywhere. Ryan wears the trendiest clothes and his hair is always styled perfectly. Perhaps this is why *People* magazine called Ryan one of its "50 Most Beautiful People," and why E! Online named him one of the "20 Young Guns Under 30 Who Hold Hollywood's Future in Their Hands."

Originally from Atlanta, Georgia, Ryan now lives and works full-time in Los Angeles. Some of his other hosting credits have included *The Billboard Awards, Radio Music Awards, EXTRA Weekends*, E!'s *Talk Soup*, NBC's Saturday Night Movie series, the Sci-Fi channel's *The New Edge, An Evening at the Academy Awards*, and ESPN shows. This past New Year's Eve, he also hosted FOX's televised festivities from Times Square in New York City.

This Spring, Ryan will launch his own clothing line, featuring some of the ultra-trendy T-shirts he's worn this past season on the show.

Simon Cowell

Mean, obnoxious, rude, outspoken, arrogant, and brutally honest are just a few of the ways judge Simon Cowell is often described. He's the *American Idol* judge who always tells it like it is, often shocking viewers and contestants alike.

While the contestants don't always enjoy hearing what Simon has to say, he's typically extremely accurate in his assessment of each performance. After all, for over 20 years, he's been an executive at BMG Music, one of the largest record labels in the world.

Aside from his judging duties on *American Idol*, Simon is also a judge on the British version of *American Idol*, called *Pop Idol*.

When he's not tearing apart a contestant's performance, Simon can often be found on the *American Idol* set either flirting or arguing with Paula Abdul, or somehow making fun of Ryan Seacrest. It's all in a day's work for this popular *American Idol* judge.

In his own unique way, Simon provides controversy, entertainment, and shock value to every episode of *American Idol*, which is why he's the judge who everyone loves to hate.

Randy Jackson

Ryan Seacrest claims to seldom understand what Randy is saying, but if you're a contestant and Randy calls you a "dawg," chances are you're in good shape. Speaking of being in good shape, Randy continues to show off his healthier new look this season, after successfully losing a significant amount of weight.

This *American Idol* judge has worked as a music producer on over 1,200 albums, for some of the biggest names in the record biz, like Mariah Carey, Madonna, Destiny's Child, Elton John, Celine Dion, Aretha Franklin, and Whitney Houston.

Having worked as an A&R executive with Columbia and MCA Records, this Grammy Award-winning producer knows exactly what it takes to become a pop superstar and create chart-topping hits.

In addition to producing music, Randy has also written *What's Up Dawg?: How To Become a Superstar in the Music Business*, plus he has worked with vocal coach to the stars, Gary Catona, on an instructional DVD for singers, called *Gary Catona's Voice Builder*.

Paula Abdul

On *American Idol*, Paula is typically Simon's alter-ego. She's friendly, supportive, compassionate, and considerate of the contestant's feelings. Prior to taking her seat at the famous judges' table, Paula herself was an incredibly successful pop recording artist, dancer, and choreographer. She's had six #1 hits, is responsible for selling well over 30 million albums worldwide, and has appeared in or choreographed countless music videos. For Janet Jackson, Paula choreographed the music videos for "When I Think of You," "Nasty," and "What Have You Done for Me Lately."

Always dressed like she just stepped off a fashion show runway, Paula has also become a savvy business woman, with her own successful jewelry line, called Innergy, plus a clothing line, called Skirtz.

Each piece in Paula's jewelry line is inscribed with the phrase, "When you wish upon a star, you might just become one." This is valuable advice she often shares with *American Idol*'s contestants. As a "good luck" gift, each of the Top 24 finalists this season received a bracelet and a necklace with this inscription as a gift from Paula.

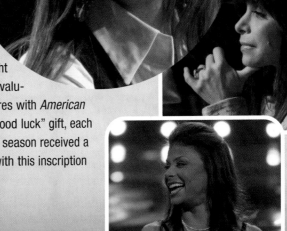

Less than two hours after Ryan wrapped up the semi-final rounds of competition on live television by announcing this season's Top 12 finalists, those who made the cut were taken to a glamorous red-carpet party at the Pacific Design Center in Hollywood. FOX threw this gala event in order to congratulate this season's finalists and formally introduce them to the media.

The Top 12 Celebrate Their Success

This was a star-studded, invitation-only event that was also attended by celebrities from FOX's other shows, such as *The O.C.*, *24*, *The Sketch Show*, *MadTV*, and *Life On a Stick*. Dozens of reporters, photographers, and television news crews from across the country enjoyed rubbing elbows with the stars and the *American Idol* finalists.

At the Pacific Design Center on Melrose Avenue in Hollywood, hundreds of lucky guests gathered to attend the gala party.

Lindsey was incredibly excited to be an honored guest at this event.

Here's what the party room looked like just minutes before the guests arrived.

As party preparations were happening inside, dozens of reporters lined the red carpet outside as they waited for the special guests to arrive.

Cast members from FOX's *Life On A Stick* were among the first celebrities to stroll down the red carpet.

As they walked down the red carpet, *American Idol*'s own Michael Orland and Dorian Holly fielded reporters' questions and discussed their thoughts about this season's Top 12 finalists.

Amy Yasbeck, "Michelle" from *Life On A Stick*, did a few interviews and allowed photographers to snap photos as she entered the party.

Season 3 Top 12 finalist LaToya London is now working as a reporter for *E! News*. She kept busy interviewing the celebrities as they walked by. Just one year earlier, LaToya was celebrating making it into the *American Idol* Top 12. In addition to reporting for E!, she's currently putting the finishing touches on her own solo album.

Before the Top 12 finalists arrived, Ryan Seacrest paved the way on the red carpet and was quickly swarmed by reporters.

Vocal coach Debra Byrd looked beautiful as she strolled down the red carpet.

Inside, the party quickly filled up with excited guests. This was an invitation-only event.

The O.C.'s Olivia Wilde ("Alex") attended the party because she's a huge *American Idol* fan.

When the finalists arrived, the reporters took turns interviewing them. Check out Anwar chatting with a reporter from one of the FOX television affiliates.

Nadia had a chance to speak with Mark Steines from *Entertainment Tonight.*

Kimberly Caldwell, a Top 12 finalist from Season 2, now works as a reporter for the *TV Guide Channel.* On the red carpet, she met up with LaToya London (who was working as a reporter for *E! News*), and they interviewed each other.

Nadia looked glamorous on the red carpet. Having the chance to attend this party was a bonus to the incredible excitement she was already feeling after making it into the Top 12.

Constantine showed off his sense of humor as he modeled an official Justin Guarini T-shirt as part of his outfit. The key-shaped necklace he wore comes from I.D. Jewelry, which makes trendy jewelry that dozens of Hollywood's biggest stars are currently wearing.

Anthony looked right at home being interviewed by several reporters at once. Everyone kept asking him how it felt to be compared to Clay Aiken. While Anthony has a deep respect for Clay and is honored by the comparison, he personally doesn't see too much similarity between Clay and himself.

Inside, the party was so crowded at times, that it was difficult to move around. Can you spot the former *American Idol* finalist who seems to be lost in the crowd?

Lindsey looked more like a glamorous movie star than a singer as she posed for the cameras.

Vonzell brought a special guest to the party...her dad.

Once inside the party, the 12 finalists had a chance to mingle with the guests and enjoy the festivities. Check out Constantine talking with Susan Slamer and a few other guests at the party.

After the party, the finalists returned to their hotel to get a good night's sleep.

Mario enjoyed the party, but less than three days later, he suddenly withdrew from the competition and gave up his spot in the Top 12. He was ultimately replaced by Nikko Smith, who was voted off the show during the third round of semi-finals, which took place about one hour before this party began.

The morning after the party, the 12 finalists began preparing for the first show in this all-new round of the competition. Now the stakes were much higher. Preparations began Thursday at 8:00 AM on the set, where the Top 12 finalists participated in several early-morning photo shoots before rehearsals.

While the party was taking place, the old *American Idol* set was torn down. A massive construction effort to build the incredible new set for the show got underway on stage 36 of CBS Television Center. Hundreds of people worked around the clock to finish building the set in time for Tuesday's show.

ANTHONY FEDOROV

The Inside Scoop

Working as a performer several nights a week at a restaurant called Tatiana in Brooklyn, New York and being a college student at the same time kept 19-year-old Anthony Fedorov pretty busy prior to auditioning for *American Idol*. This hectic schedule did, however, help to prepare him for what he's been experiencing as a Top 12 finalist.

While in high school, Anthony participated in a wide range of sports, including basketball, hockey, and football. These days, however, he stays in shape by working out daily. He also enjoys running and swimming.

Life seems pretty sweet right now for the Top 12 finalist who manages to belt out power ballads week after week while effortlessly winning over the hearts of teenage girls everywhere. As a child, however, Anthony never dreamed of becoming a singer. In fact, at age five, all he wanted to do was to be able to speak.

> **When I feel strongly about something, I put my heart into it.**

Idol Fast Facts

Hometown ....Trevose, PA
Audition City.........Cleveland, OH
Birthday.....................May 4, 1985
Sign.......................................Taurus

ON THE PERSONAL SIDE...

Favorite Recording Artists:	Marc Anthony, Michael Bolton, Brian Adams, Brian McKnight, and Stevie Wonder
Favorite Food:	Sushi
Favorite Color:	Blue
Favorite TV Show:	*The Fresh Prince of Bel Air*
Favorite Movie:	"I like comedies, but I don't currently have a favorite."
Favorite Subject in School:	European History
Worst Subject in School:	Math
Pets:	"I have no pets right now, but I dream of having a dog someday"
Hobbies:	Watching and playing sports, fishing, reading, and spending time with his close friends

Anthony was born with an abnormal growth on his vocal cords which prevented him from being able to speak. At age five, he underwent an operation that resulted in a tracheotomy. Doctors needed to cut a small hole in his throat to help him breathe. After this operation, the doctors again believed Anthony's ability to speak would be limited at best. He proved them very wrong.

Through specialized therapy, Anthony not only was able to speak, he eventually strengthened his vocal chords enough to sing, even reaching and sustaining extremely difficult notes. For Anthony, earning a spot in the Top 12 is an incredible accomplishment. The pride he feels can be seen in the smile that's present every single minute of every day that he's on the set. "I'm so happy to be here," is a phrase he utters countless times each day to everyone on the show's production team.

In addition to having a wonderful voice, Anthony is a self-taught pianist and guitar player. He's an extremely outgoing person with an awesome sense of humor. "I'm an open and honest person who is very passionate about everything I do in life. When I feel strongly about something, I put my heart into it. My biggest treasure and my biggest flaw, however, is that I always see the good in people and I keep faith alive," explained Anthony.

After making it through the Cleveland auditions, Anthony was, of course, invited to Hollywood for the next phase of the audition process. "The week in Hollywood was a fun experience. One of our assignments was performing in a group, which was not something I'd ever done before. It was a learning experience for me. When the judges told me I'd earned a spot in the Top 24, my life passed before my eyes. I was so happy," recalled Anthony, who said he's been keeping a detailed diary of his experiences each day that he's been involved with the show.

No matter how much pressure the finalists are put under, Anthony seems to take it all in stride as he remains focused on simply offering up the best performances he can muster. "Partway through the semi-finals, I went through an emotionally challenging few days, but I pulled myself out of it and managed to refocus my mind. I was unsure of what was happening and that scared me. Normally, I am a very mentally and emotionally stable person," said Anthony, who has never had any formal vocal training to be a singer.

Behind-the-Scenes Moments

Anthony rehearsed with Michael Orland and Dorian Holly.

While Anthony sipped his tea, he and music supervisor Susan Slamer had a brief chat during a rehearsal.

Here's Anthony relaxing in the contestants' lounge and creating some artwork on an Etch-A-Sketch.

Just moments before he stepped onstage during the semi-finals, Anthony looked totally calm, but was really very excited.

Anthony got the royal makeover treatment from the hair and make-up team.

When asked about his image, Anthony fears that he sometimes comes off as being very goofy. He's often compared to former *American Idol* runner-up Clay Aiken in terms of his look and talent. "I am honored to be compared to Clay, although I want people to see me for who I am. In many ways, I am different from Clay. I hope people who watch the show will discover this about me as the season progresses. What you see on stage is exactly who I am," he said. "To avoid getting caught up in the stress and pressure, I've made a conscious decision not to think about my image."

When he made it into the Top 12, one of the things Anthony was looking forward to was working with Dean Banowetz and his team of hairstylists. "I've wanted to try new things with my hair for a long time. Now, I'll have the chance to experiment with some new and different looks," added Anthony.

These three audience members easily picked out their favorite *American Idol* finalist!

During many of his breaks, Anthony spends time in the contestants' lounge playing the keyboards.

On March 9th, after being voted into the Top 12, Anthony had a blast being interviewed by dozens of reporters at the FOX party in Hollywood.

Anthony is proud to be among this season's Top 12 finalists.

For years, Anthony has worked hard to constantly improve his voice and perfect his skills as a performer. To those who have been voting for him throughout the season, he said, "I am grateful for all of the support I've received. I know that without all of you, I would not be here. I am grateful for all of the love and support. I am so lucky. This whole experience doesn't seem real."

During the first few weeks of the Top 12 competition, Anthony has been both praised and berated by the three judges. "Deep down, I truly believe Simon is a friendly and nice guy. I hope I get to see that side of him. Except for when we're on stage performing, we seldom see the judges and have had little time to get to know them personally. To win this competition, I believe I have the talent to succeed. What will be required, however, is that I remain mentally strong, no matter what happens," said Anthony, who has become good friends with many of the finalists.

Performance Highlights

Whenever Anthony steps on the *American Idol* stage, you know an emotion-filled and power-packed performance is about to take place.

Anthony credits some of his success in life, as well as on the show, to the love and support he receives from his girlfriend. "We met almost two years ago at a singing contest. Neither of us won, but we got our prize," he said.

Whatever happens during the *American Idol* season, Anthony is prepared to move his career forward and looks at his work on the show as being an incredible learning experience and an amazing launching pad for whatever will come next.

"My life has changed dramatically since I first auditioned for *American Idol*. This continues to be a dream come true for me," he concluded. "For someone thinking about auditioning for Season 5 of *American Idol*, make sure you stay true to yourself and respect those around you. Having the right attitude is extremely important."

When he sings, Anthony often dedicates his performances to his fans, because he's truly grateful for all of their support.

Anthony's stunning good looks and charm, as well as his voice, have earned him many votes from the show's female viewers.

For Anthony, performing on the *American Idol* stage is a dream come true.

ANWAR ROBINSON

The Inside Scoop

Almost every aspect of Anwar's life is totally dedicated to music. For his full-time job, he works as a music teacher for middle school students in New Jersey. All of his students are extremely excited to see their teacher as a finalist on *American Idol* and have been very supportive of his success and popularity.

When Anwar was getting ready to come to Los Angeles to compete on the show, he packed his clothing along with a teddy bear named "Tender Heart," which was a good luck gift from his seventh-grade students. He can almost always be seen on stage wearing a wristband given to him by his best friend.

"
Everything I do is music-related. I love music.
"

Idol Fast Facts

Hometown:.................................Newark, NJ
Audition City:.....................Washington, DC
Birthday:...................................April 21, 1979
Sign:...Taurus

ON THE PERSONAL SIDE...

Favorite Recording Artists:	Stevie Wonder, Aretha Franklin, Patti LaBelle, and Brian McKnight
Favorite Food:	Smoked salmon
Favorite Color:	Tan
Favorite TV Show:	*Three's Company*
Favorite Movie:	*Be Cool*
Favorite Subject in School:	Music
Worst Subject in School:	History
Pets:	None
Hobbies:	Playing piano, shopping, and following the latest fashion trends

"I am a very kind and sensitive individual who really cares about the well-being of other people," explained Anwar. "I am also hard-working and do what's necessary to always get the job done. I think what sets me apart from the other finalists is all of the time I have spent studying and teaching music. Everything I do is music-related. I love music."

Before auditioning for *American Idol*, Anwar knew in his heart that he had talent. When he first arrived in Hollywood for the final phase of auditions, however, he became somewhat intimidated by the other incredibly talented guys who would be his competitors.

"My respect for the other semi-finalists quickly grew when I heard each of them sing. I believe that God has given me all of my gifts and my musical ability. I credit Him, first and foremost, for everything that's happened to me," said Anwar, who thinks about connecting with the audience and having fun whenever he's on stage.

"I don't think about the judges or what they're thinking about me when I am performing on stage. Initially, I thought it was the judges who would make me nervous, but they don't. I don't pay too much attention to them. I think that's one of the reasons why I have been able to stay pretty calm so far," explained Anwar, who is doing his best to get plenty of sleep and eat well during the competition.

Like all the Top 12 finalists, Anwar has his own strategies for staying in the competition. "I have no idea how to win over fans or TV viewers. All I know how to do is perform and make great music. I know music. I love music and I am willing to share my music with whoever will listen. As we progress further in the final weeks of competition, I am just being myself and choosing songs I love and that I can make my own. I believe that my song choices need to speak to people. A song isn't worth singing if it doesn't have anything to say or if the singer can't communicate with his audience by singing it," he added.

Anwar considers himself to be a "balladeer to the hilt," although he looks forward to performing other genres of music as well. "I love singing power ballads," he says. "In terms of the theme shows, I would love the producers to choose a 'big band' or 'Barry Manilow' theme, like they did last season, because I'd love to sing 'Copacabana.' That's a fun song that I love to perform."

Behind-the-Scenes Moments

During a break from rehearsals, Anwar and David sang together. Anwar is an awesome keyboard player as well as an accomplished music teacher.

Anwar rehearsed on the *American Idol* stage so he could nail those difficult notes and impress the judges.

After listening to Lindsey and Carrie perform each week, Anwar has acquired a taste for country music. "At first, I thought some of the other finalists were a shoe-in to win this competition. Now, I realize that we all have our unique strengths and some-thing to offer. That makes this a pretty fair competition," said Anwar, who believes that being a teacher has taught him how to be incredibly patient and understanding.

"Knowing how to maintain total calmness within myself is an extremely beneficial skill. I also really appreciate the lessons I am learning from Michael Orland and Dorian Holly. Any good teacher worth their grain of salt will appreciate being taught from other people and being a great learner," explained Anwar.

Part of being in the *American Idol* finals involves working with the show's fashion consultant, make-up artists, and hairstylists. Through this experience, Anwar hopes to learn what appeals to audiences and incorporate this newly acquired information into his personal style. He refuses, however, to make drastic changes

Anwar and Nadia looked through *The Billboard Book of Number 1 Hits* and discussed their upcoming song selections.

In the contestants' lounge, Anwar caught up on his reading.

to his personality or appearance. "The last thing I want is to look in the mirror and not be able to recognize myself when this whole experience is over," explained Anwar, who is a little apprehensive about becoming famous so quickly as a result of appearing on the show.

Anwar believes he is living his life to fulfill a personal mission. "My mission is to respect music to a point where it is recognized as a vital art form among all human life, without exalting it above the human spirit." In other words, he wants to teach music in a way that it helps people appreciate themselves and the world around them.

Through participating on *American Idol*, Anwar has discovered he's a lot stronger as a person than he originally thought. He looks forward to sharing his music with as many people as possible through *American Idol* and through whatever opportunities arise in the future.

Performance Highlights

Anwar always looks at home on stage.

During the semi-finals, Anwar needed to impress the judges as well as the home audience in order to win those all-important votes.

Anwar's mellow and soothing voice quickly wins over television viewers everywhere.

Anwar bundles a ton of emotion into his performances, which helps to make them memorable.

There's already a "Prince of Pop," but with his consistently impressive performances, Anwar could eventually become the new king of mid-tempo ballads.

The Inside Scoop

Before he auditioned for *American Idol*, 29-year-old Bo would have describe himself as a "gigging musician." He was also the manager of a guitar store in Birmingham, Alabama. Now, his life has become a lot more exciting. After all, he's one of the oldest contestants in this season's Top 12.

When Bo auditioned for *American Idol* and needed to take time off to travel to Hollywood for the final phase of auditions, he was fired from his job. "They said I should choose between *American Idol* and my job. I took a huge gamble and went to the auditions. I had no idea I'd ultimately make it into the Top 12. I am very glad I made the right decision," explained Bo. "I never thought I'd be sitting here in Hollywood, within my own dressing room at *American Idol*."

Bo Bice

> I had no idea I'd ultimately make it into the Top 12.

Idol Fast Facts

Hometown...........................Birmingham, AL
Audition City ....Orlando, FL
Birthday ....November 1, 1975
Sign..Scorpio

ON THE PERSONAL SIDE...

Favorite Recording Artists:	**Jim Croce, the Allman Brothers Band, the Eagles, and Willie Nelson**
Favorite Food:	**Italian**
Favorite Color:	**Green**
Favorite TV Show:	*Seinfeld*
Favorite Movie:	*The Shawshank Redemption*
Favorite Subjects in School:	**Band and Choir**
Worst Subject in School:	**"Anything that wasn't band or choir."**
Pets:	**Two dogs, three cats, and two aquatic turtles**
Hobbies:	**Recording and writing music in his home studio**

Bo enjoys listening to all types of music, but if he could only have one song to listen to for the rest of his life, he said it would be Jim Croce's "Time In A Bottle." Growing up, Bo listened to many music genres, however. "I try not to discriminate between any styles of music. Music is true creativity. If I discriminate against creativity, I believe it will hinder my own creativity," said Bo, who also enjoys watching rugby.

While he was growing up, Bo spent five years living in France with his family. "Annecy, France and Dublin, Ireland are my two favorite places in the world to visit," he said. These days, however, Bo enjoys spending virtually all of his free time working in his home studio writing, recording, and producing music. He's also involved with his church's band.

One of Bo's activities that started out as a hobby and quickly transformed into a small business is offering guitar and piano lessons to young people. "In this lifetime, I believe we are put here to help make the next generation better. To be able to pass on what I know about music to younger kids is extremely fun and rewarding. It's something that I cherish," explained Bo.

Since coming to Hollywood to compete on *American Idol*, Bo has received many phone calls from his young music students. "They're not calling to wish me luck, necessarily. What they want to know is when I'll be home so we can resume their music lessons. That warms my heart and makes me feel like my life has a purpose," said Bo proudly.

As a musician, Bo plays the bass, acoustical, and electric guitar, piano, saxophone, and the harmonica. He learned how to play saxophone when he was a member of his high school's band. He taught himself how to play the rest of the instruments. "I got my first guitar from my mom and dad for my ninth birthday," he added.

If you're wondering what Bo is like in real life, he considers himself to be fun-loving, easygoing and a guy who would give someone the shirt off his back in a snow storm.

"I auditioned for *American Idol* as a result of a bet with my mother after we learned they raised the eligibility age to 28. She dared me to audition for the show and I dared her to come with me to the auditions. She hopped in our truck and drove to Orlando with me. She then camped out with me for two nights as I waited to audition. Those nights sleeping on the cement floor in the convention center were like having a slumber party with thousands of people," recalled Bo.

Bo knows how important it is to select the songs he performs each week; each song must allow him to showcase who he

Behind-the-Scenes Moments

Bo and Vonzell waited for their tea to be served as they relaxed at the Grove shopping mall near the *American Idol* set.

Talk about multi-tasking... Bo checks his email and plays the harmonica at the same time.

To help him relax, Bo enjoys playing the guitar.

is as a performer in under two minutes. "I need to pick songs with lyrics that will allow me to sell myself to television viewers. I look for songs that communicate to me and make me go 'wow' when I hear them. I am always being myself when I perform on *American Idol.* I only perform songs I truly love," he said.

When it comes to rocker stereotypes, Bo doesn't necessarily fit the mold. Sure, he has long hair and a few tattoos, but there's a lot more to him than what you might expect. "There is no label that perfectly describes my music and my performance abilities. I was raised on a diverse background of music and I enjoy listening to and performing many types of music. No matter what genre of music you select, I can easily find songs I can sing well that I really love," said Bo, who said he believes it's important to be able to perform many genres of music in order to be a well-rounded performer and recording artist.

When Bo made it into the Top 12, he was in awe not only that he'd made it this far in the competition, but also at the caliber of talent his fellow finalists possess. "Everyone in the Top 12 is amazingly talented. It's very hard to see someone voted off the show each week. I have made some really good friends here. It's

A few days after arriving in Hollywood for the semi-finals, Bo got a new tattoo on his chest in honor of the occasion.

Bo relaxes before his performance.

Bo and Constantine chatted with *American Idol*'s music supervisor Susan Slamer.

hard to see one of them headed home after every Wednesday night's results show," said Bo, who focuses on the studio audience when he performs on the *American Idol* stage, as opposed to the almost 30 million people watching at home.

One thing Bo wants everyone to know about him is that he is truly grateful for the experience he's having on *American Idol*. "I have been playing music and trying to make it in this business since I was 14. I never dreamed I'd perform on a show like *American Idol* and then be recognized by people across the country almost overnight. Being recognized when I go out in public is a

wonderful feeling," explained Bo, who really looks forward to meeting as many of his fans as he can.

Whenever Bo performs on stage or travels away from home, he carries in his pocket a small felt sack containing a handful of lucky trinkets and mementos given to him by friends and loved ones.

To help him deal with the many pressures involved with being on *American Idol*, Bo relies on his pastor to send him inspirational scripture which helps him stay focused and better able to

Performance Highlights

Bo and Constantine are Season 4's two rockers!

Bo rocked the audience during the first round of semi-finals.

meditate. He also enjoys playing the guitar to help him relax. "One of the first things I did when I got to Los Angeles was to buy a new guitar," said Bo.

Bo believes that being a "gigging musician" for so many years prior to appearing on *American Idol* has helped him deal with all of the pressure this show puts on the finalists.

When asked what he thinks it'll take to win this year's *American Idol* competition, Bo was quick to respond, "Compared to people like Carrie and Nikko, I don't think I have a chance to win this thing. I've had my bags packed every single Wednesday night. I am not a pessimistic person. I am very grateful to be here. I am in the Top 12 out of over 100,000 people. I am honored that so many people watching this show appreciate my music. Whatever happens from this point forward, I am very proud of my accomplishment. I know this is just the beginning to the rest of my life. I would love to stay here on the show as long as the viewers will keep voting for me."

Could this 29-year-old rocker become the next *American Idol*?

Bo knows how to rock the crowd.

Bo says he's extremely honored to be part of the Top 12.

CARRIE UNDERWOOD

Carrie Underwood has become known on *American Idol* as the innocent farm girl from Oklahoma. In real life, that's exactly who she is. At 22, she's currently a full-time student at Northeastern State University, although she had to take a semester off in order to participate in *American Idol*. In school, Carrie has been studying mass communication with an emphasis on television journalism, which is something she hopes to pursue as a career.

Carrie is drop-dead gorgeous. Aside from her stunning good looks, she's also a talented singer and an extremely compassionate person.

> "I want people to know that I really am a fun-loving, small-town country girl."

Idol Fast Facts

Hometown: ....Chocotah, OK
Audition City:.........................St. Louis, MO
Birthday:................................March 10, 1983
Sign:..Pisces

ON THE PERSONAL SIDE...

Favorite Recording Artists:	**Martina McBride and and George Michael**
Favorite Food:	**Pizza**
Favorite Color:	**Blue**
Favorite TV Show:	*Star Trek: The Next Generation*
Favorite Movie:	*Nightmare on Elm Street* **and all horror movies**
Favorite Subject in School:	**English**
Worst Subject in School:	**Math**
Pets:	**Two cats and two dogs**
Hobbies:	**Playing guitar, watching movies, and hanging out with her sorority sisters from college**

"I am a pretty quiet person who isn't too emotional. Once people get to know me, however, they see that I'm a lot of fun to be around. Initially, I am shy around new people. One thing I'm definitely not is an airhead!" she explained.

When Carrie heard about the *American Idol* auditions in St. Louis, she had to convince her mom to drive her there; she lives almost 500 miles from the nearest audition city.

"Once my mother agreed to drive me, we had to wait there forever. I had to perform the night before the auditions, so after my performance, we hopped in the car and drove all night. I was then one of the last people to audition in St. Louis, so I had to wait for many hours. I was so tired when I finally got to audition. I'm not sure what they saw in me, but I am grateful for this opportunity," explained Carrie.

During the Hollywood auditions, like many of the contestants, at one point Carrie panicked and forgot her lyrics when she was performing in front of the judges. Because she had done so well previously, the judges gave her a second chance and she ultimately earned a spot in the Top 24. From there, America voted to put her into the Top 12.

When she was packing to come to Los Angeles, Carrie brought along some photos of her friends, family, and pets. She also packed a teddy bear given to her by her boyfriend. "What I miss most about being home is being able to lay around, relax, and do absolutely nothing. On *American Idol*, we're always busy. There's so little time to relax. I also really miss my parents and friends, but I speak with them on the phone all the time," added Carrie, who is still a bit intimidated when performing in front of Simon, Paula, and Randy.

"Every Wednesday night during the results show, I always look back at my previous performances and think about what I could have done differently or better. I try to second guess myself. The results shows are so emotional," said Carrie. "During the actual live results shows, all I can really do is sit there and hope enough people voted for me to keep me in the competition."

From the beginning of the competition, the judges and producers have stressed the importance of song selection. Each week, the judges have also consistently complimented Carrie because she continues to be true to herself in terms of the songs she performs and the outfits she wears. While her hairstyles have changed from week to week, Carrie isn't trying to be anyone other than herself—the 22-year-old girl from Oklahoma who loves country music.

Behind-the-Scenes Moments

The day after making it into the Top 12, Carrie celebrated her birthday on the set. Her fellow contestants and the producers gave her a cake and sang "happy birthday."

At the mall, Carrie had a blast trying on colorful hats.

"As we learn the theme for each week's show, I try to pick songs that I already know. I don't want to learn an entirely new song in three days and then have to sing it on live television in front of so many people. As for what I wear, I'm never going to wear anything that's too revealing. I'm very self-conscious. I'm not too good at picking out outfits, so I rely on advice from friends," explained Carrie, who has enjoyed working with Miles Siggins, *American Idol*'s wardrobe and fashion consultant.

One high point during the season was when Carrie celebrated her birthday on the *American Idol* set. After rehearsals, the crew and her fellow contestants celebrated by presenting Carrie with a birthday cake.

Here, Lindsey, Nadia, and Carrie chat on stage during a commercial break.

Carrie loves to shop for jewelry and fashion accessories.

Carry always looks amazing, whether she wears her hair straight or curly.

Carrie gets her make-up done before going on stage.

As she makes it further in the competition, Carrie looks forward to having viewers get to know her better. "People only get to see so much of us each week on the show, but I want people to know that I really am a fun-loving, small-town country girl," she added. "While you won't typically see me get emotional on television, I often go back to my room and let my emotions loose when I'm alone. I don't spent a lot of time thinking about how I am going to win this competition. All I concern myself with is what I'm going to do for my next performance in order to stay on the show for an additional week. I just try to do my very best."

Carrie is quick to admit that if she hadn't made it onto *American Idol*, she probably never would have left home to come to Los Angeles. "Being away from home, I've learned a lot about myself and the music business. I know my life will never go back to the way it was before I left home. What the future holds is very exciting, but scary at the same time," she concluded. "As much as I love music, I have a true passion for animals. I don't know what I'd do if I didn't have both music and animals in my life."

Performance Highlights

Carrie loves to show off her country charm when she's performing.

Carrie was delighted when she got good news from the judges after a performance.

When Ryan spouts off the phone number viewers can use to vote for Carrie, who could resist voting for this utterly charming country girl with a power-packed voice?

During the early stages of the semi-finals, Carrie demonstrated she can consistently hit those powerful notes.

You can always count on Carrie to offer an up-beat and fun performance, no matter what song she's singing.

Carrie makes her presence known when she's on the *American Idol* stage. She may be soft-spoken during conversations, but on stage, she can really belt out those notes.

CONSTANTINE MAROULIS

The Inside Scoop

Since graduating from college in 2002, Constantine has been working virtually non-stop as a singer and actor. Prior to auditioning for *American Idol*, the 29-year-old starred in the lead role of "Roger" in the touring company of the hit Broadway show *Rent*.

Constantine is also the lead singer of the rock group "Pray for the Soul of Betty" (www.prayforthesoulofbetty.com) and has toured extensively with the group. "I'm a full-time artist and musician, but I've also done some bartending and a bit of work in real estate," said the die-hard New York Yankees baseball fan.

"With 'Pray for the Soul of Betty,' I've traveled throughout America and to a handful of other countries. The most exciting place we performed was Japan. Tokyo is the most amazing place. I was a total tourist during the entire visit. I took several bus tours. We've also been to Ireland, Greece, Holland, plus several other countries, but I definitely love America the best. I really appreciate small towns and Americana at its best," Constantine said.

"

...nothing could really prepare someone for the experience of competing on this show. It's so intense.

"

Idol Fast Facts

Hometown .... New York, NY
Audition City .... Washington, DC
Birthday .... September 17, 1975
Sign .... Virgo

ON THE PERSONAL SIDE...

Favorite Recording Artists:	**Sam Cook, Nat King Cole, Frank Sinatra, Led Zeppelin, The Doors, Guns N' Roses, and Nirvana**
Favorite Food:	**Pasta**
Favorite Color:	**Blue**
Favorite TV Show:	***Law & Order***
Favorite Movie:	***The Godfather***
Favorite Subject in School:	**Music**
Worst Subject in School:	**Math**
Pets:	**A dog**
Hobbies:	**Writing music, watching sports (baseball), hiking, and travel**

"I am a cultured, driven, well-balanced, spiritual young artist who is hungry to learn more about my craft and who always strives to better himself," explained Constantine, who has been dubbed one of the two "rockers" among this season's *American Idol* finalists.

He added, "It was a good friend of mine who insisted that I audition for *American Idol*. She thought I'd make a good addition to the show. I had never actually watched the show before, so I didn't know what to expect. My friend convinced me to go to the audition. Now, I can't thank her enough. This show provides me with an incredible opportunity to go out on stage and do my thing in front of millions of people every week. What greater opportunity could anyone ask for?"

It was during the summer of 2003 that Constantine helped form his rock group, "Pray for the Soul of Betty." The group started off in New York, but quickly gained popularity as it began touring outside the metropolitan area. "I was working with the group when I landed the role in *Rent*. Instead of giving up the band, I figured out a way to do both at the same time. I took the band on the road, so in the evening I performed in *Rent*, then at night, 'Pray for the Soul of Betty' performed at local clubs and theaters in the cities where the touring company of *Rent* traveled to," recalled Constantine. "We traveled to more than 30 cities and piggybacked off of the *Rent* tour. It was a great experience. During that time, we really came together as a band."

If you're wondering where the band name came from, Constantine explained "Pray for the Soul of Betty" is something he and his fellow group members like to keep to themselves. "The name symbolizes a lot of things. What's interesting about the members of the group is that we were all living in New York City when we formed the group, but we all represent different nationalities. This eclectic makeup gives our original music a unique sound, yet we stay true to our musical roots as an old-fashion New York rock-and-roll band. When we were thinking up a name for the group, we didn't want anything that sounded contrived," said Constantine, who hinted that Betty was an actual person.

Constantine hopes to set the record straight about his involvement with "Pray for the Soul of Betty." While he didn't tell his group members when he auditioned for *American Idol*, he remains extremely close friends with the other people in the group and looks forward to eventually working with them again once his *American Idol* experience ends. "I have an amazing bond with the guys in my group. That will never die," he explained. "We will always be able to make music together, but hopefully, I will also do well here, on *American Idol*."

Behind-the-Scenes Moments

While relaxing on the floor of the Red Room, Constantine responded to personal e-mails from his handheld wireless PDA.

Constantine modeled his official Justin Guarini T-shirt as he posed for the cameras at the FOX party. This Top 12 finalist maintained his rocker image, yet showed off his sense of humor.

Check out Constantine's first time sitting in the make-up chair. He doesn't look too happy about having to wear make-up, but it's something all performers have to endure.

The hair and make-up team working on *American Idol* always make Constantine look his best when he's performing.

Like Bo, on the surface, Constantine perfectly fits the stereotype of a "rocker," yet, when you get to know him, it's easy to see that there's a lot more to this performer. During one of the Top 12 competition shows, Constantine showed off his sense of humor when he performed "I Think I Love You"—a song made famous by the television show *The Partridge Family*. It was hardly a rock-and-roll song and something few people expected Constantine would ever perform. He's also been seen wearing a Justin Guarini T-shirt when he makes publicity appearances and does interviews in conjunction with *American Idol*.

Anyone who spends time with Constantine will quickly discover he's kind, thoughtful, extremely talented, intelligent and very down-to-earth. He also has a strong appreciation for all genres of music, not just rock.

Even during rehearsals, Constantine belts out his vocals.

After an important rehearsal, executive producers Nigel Lythgoe and Ken Warwick offer Constantine a pat on the back.

Ryan sits with Constantine, Nadia, and the other nervous contestants during a dress rehearsal for that night's results show.

Constantine describes himself as an artist, not as a rocker. "I feel like I am a versatile performer. I hope the fans of *American Idol* don't pigeonhole me just as a rocker. I love rock and roll and the attitude that goes along with it. On *American Idol*, I am, however, looking forward to the theme weeks so I can challenge myself to perform other types of music and showcase what I am really capable of. I grew up listening to all types of music and have a strong appreciation for all music," he said.

What Constantine really likes about *American Idol* this season is that each of the Top 12 finalists is very different. "Each one of us has something very unique to bring to the competition. My work with 'Pray for the Soul of Betty' and *Rent* has given me some experience which has definitely helped me during the *American Idol* competition, but nothing could really prepare someone for the experience of competing on this show. It's that intense," he added. "This show is all about performing different styles of music that we have to learn very quickly. Working with my band and on *Rent*, I had to perform the same material over-and-over, several nights per week."

Performance Highlights

At the same time, Bo and Constantine discovered that they both made it into the Top 12.

When he performs, Constantine often wears a necklace the he originally wore on stage when he starred in the show *Rent*.

The 29-year-old rocker is a man of mystery and of many talents. He's a musician, songwriter, actor, singer, and all-around performer.

Check out Constantine during week one of the semi-finals. He quickly stood out from his fellow contestants.

Constantine shows America what rock and roll is all about!

Constantine will rock your world when he's on stage.

JESSICA SIERRA

The Inside Scoop

Jessica Sierra loves kids. Before she auditioned for *American Idol*, the 19-year-old worked as a nanny for a family with two young kids. "My life is now dedicated to my music, but if I need to earn an income while I am trying to pursue my music career, I'd definitely work as a nanny again," said Jessica, who experienced a family tragedy just after auditioning for *American Idol*.

Growing up, Jessica was raised primarily by her father and grandparents, all of whom sat in the *American Idol* audience week after week supporting the Top 12 finalist. Her birth mother wasn't part of Jessica's life until she became a teenager. After the two started to get close, however, Jessica's mother passed away rather suddenly.

> **Growing up, I took the opportunity to sing and perform any chance I could.**

Idol Fast Facts

Hometown	Tampa, FL
Audition City	Orlando, FL
Birthday	November 11, 1985
Sign	Scorpio

ON THE PERSONAL SIDE...

Favorite Recording Artists:	Elton John, Billy Joel, and a wide range of country artists
Favorite Foods:	Black beans and rice
Favorite Color:	Pink
Favorite TV Shows:	*Law & Order* and *Law & Order: SVU*
Favorite Movie:	*Napoleon Dynamite*
Favorite Subject in School:	Math
Worst Subject in School:	English
Pets:	Five dogs
Hobbies:	Line dancing, playing pool, and bowling

"My mother left when I was three. I didn't really see her again until I was 15. Just prior to leaving for the Hollywood auditions, she died rather suddenly. That was a traumatic experience," explained Jessica. According to Jessica, it's been her grandmother who has pushed Jessica to pursue singing and provided inspiration throughout her life.

"One of the greatest parts of my whole experience on *American Idol* is seeing how happy and proud my grandmother is. I am so glad my grandparents are still alive to see me on the show," said Jessica, who loves playing football with her guy friends. She's also a huge professional football fan. Her favorite team is the Tampa Bay Buccaneers.

Jessica describes herself as a fun and loving person. Although she managed to make it into the Top 12 for Season 4, Jessica originally auditioned for Season 3 in Atlanta, but didn't make it past the first phase of auditions. "When someone tells me I can't do something, that makes me all the more determined to do it and succeed. That's why I came back and auditioned again for *American Idol*. I needed to prove to myself I could do it," she said.

As a teenager, Jessica was a member of a girl group, called Entertainment Review. Even though the group disbanded a few years ago, she remains very close friends with several of the group's former members. "Growing up, I took the opportunity to sing and perform any chance I could," she added.

While Jessica can typically be found laughing and smiling, the *American Idol* results shows have been particularly difficult for her emotionally. "There are a lot of people I have gotten close to on this show. Seeing them get voted off is very difficult for me. Overall, however, this is an amazing experience. The hardest part is not knowing if you'll be sent home during each Wednesday night's show," said Jessica.

"After each results show, I am a complete emotional basket case. I want to be here and continue to move on in the competition, but at the same time, I am not afraid of getting voted off the show. Watching other people get kicked off the show is really hard for me. We're all so close to making it in the music business as a result of *American Idol*. To see this opportunity get yanked away from people I have become close to isn't easy," explained Jessica.

Behind-the-Scenes Moments

Hairstylist Ryan helped to create a new look for Jessica.

Here's Jessica rehearsing on the new *American Idol* stage.

Jessica made funny faces on the Red Room set.

Executive producer Nigel Lythgoe offered up some advice to Jessica about her upcoming performance.

"The songs I choose may not always showcase my voice the best way possible, but they're songs I have a strong attachment to or that I deeply relate to," said Jessica. "When I have an attachment to a song, it's much easier for me to put my feelings into it and make it an emotion-filled performance. For example, I sang 'Against All Odds [Take a Look at Me Now]' because that song reminded me of my mother. When I am singing, what I focus on is the lyrics of the song. I don't really think about the audience watching me."

When it comes to clothes, especially what she wears on the show, Jessica chooses outfits that she's comfortable in. "I'm not trying to convey any type of image or attitude. I dress based on my mood. Sometimes, I like to be funky and wild. Other times, I dress a bit more subdued. I like to have fun with my outfits," she said.

During a rehearsal, a more casually dressed Jessica kicked back on the *American Idol* stage.

Jessica is proud to be one of the six girls to make it into this season's Top 12.

Jessica loves to shop. During a visit to the Grove shopping mall, she dropped into Abercrombie & Fitch and couldn't leave without adding to her wardrobe.

Thus far in her life, the biggest lesson Jessica has learned is that life always goes on, despite what good or bad events transpire. "I believe it's important to pursue things you really love. For me, that's singing and performing. It sometimes takes a lot of hard work to accomplish your goals, but that's okay. It's important to stay positive and motivated about what's really important and to stay focused on your goals," explained Jessica, who describes herself as a very social person.

Jessica is at a loss for what television viewers are looking for in their next *American Idol*. "In past seasons, it's not always the best singer who wins. It's also about personality, appearance, and originality. The TV viewers like to get to know the contestants. They then vote for the person they most relate to," she said. "While many people may be afraid of Simon, I love him. I truly respect that he's brutally honest. There's nothing sugar coated about the music industry. Simon always tells it like it is. I also think he's hot!"

Performance Highlights

Anwar gives Jessica a hug when the two discovered they had made it into the Top 12.

Jessica makes her song selections based on her emotional attachment to the lyrics.

After Jessica chooses which song she'll perform, she selects an outfit to match the mood of the song and her own personal taste.

From past *American Idol* seasons, Jessica really respects Clay Aiken and Jennifer Hudson. "I also respect Fantasia because she's gone through so much to get where she is right now," concluded Jessica. "What I feel like I share with Clay, Jennifer, and Fantasia is my own personal determination to succeed on the show."

Being voted into the bottom three after the first Top 12 competition show of the season was very emotionally difficult for Jessica.

During the Top 12 shows, Jessica tries to have as much fun as possible when she's on stage performing.

Check out Jessica as she performs during the semi-finals.

LINDSEY CARDINALE

Music has always been one of Lindsey's passions, but as a sophomore in college, her academic work is gearing her toward a career in radiology. "I have always wanted to do something in a hospital, but I have never been one to handle all of the stuff that nurses do. Working as a radiologist, I can help people while working in the medical field," explained the 20-year-old *American Idol* finalist.

Lindsey mainly enjoys listening to and performing country music. Outside of her musical interests, she played softball for 11 years, both for her junior high school and for a citywide league. "I am a very outgoing person who is willing to try almost anything. It takes a lot to scare me. I'm also very tenderhearted and I really care about other people," she explained.

"
I am a strong person who can add emotion to my music.
"

Idol Fast Facts

Hometown......................Ponchatoula, LA
Audition City....................New Orleans, LA
Birthday.............................February 5, 1985
Sign...Aquarius

ON THE PERSONAL SIDE...

Favorite Recording Artists:	**Norah Jones, Julie Roberts, Sara Evens, and Allen Jackson**
Favorite Food:	**Beef stew**
Favorite Color:	**Blue**
Favorite TV Show:	***Friends***
Favorite Movies:	***The Little Mermaid* and *8 Seconds***
Favorite Subject in School:	**English**
Worst Subject in School:	**History**
Pets:	**None**
Hobbies:	**Singing and performing**

After watching *American Idol* for three seasons, Lindsey noticed that few of the contestants performed country music. She decided to take the opportunity to wow the judges with her own style of country music when she auditioned for Season 4.

"The day before the producers came to New Orleans to hold auditions, I decided to give it a try. During the Hollywood phase of the auditions, Simon said that I was giving good performances, so that boosted my confidence. It was then I realized I had a shot of making it into the Top 12," said Lindsey, who carries a small horseshoe for good luck when she performs. It was a gift from her mother.

In the past, Lindsey has performed at dozens of local fairs and festivals, as well as at countless weddings. She's also been active with choirs at both school and church. "I've been singing since I was 11 years old and have been performing everywhere that I could, although I've never had any formal training. I've also never experienced anything like *American Idol*," added Lindsey.

Lindsey admits to being intimidated when she was surrounded by hundreds of talented singers during the Hollywood phase of the auditions. She explained, "The week we spent auditioning in Hollywood was very overwhelming for me. I really enjoyed the solo performances, but some of the challenges they gave us were difficult. I didn't believe the judges when they told me I'd be in the Top 24. It didn't feel real when they told me I'd made it."

During the semi-finals and the first week of the finals, Lindsey, like all of the contestants, stayed in Los Angeles and was away from her friends and loved ones. This initially made her homesick. "I always travel with my family or friends. I come from a big family and we're very close. Being in Los Angeles all alone, I really missed sleeping in my own bed, my family, and my six really close friends. Every time I started feeling homesick, however, I thought about how *American Idol* was a once-in-a-lifetime opportunity," she said.

Unfortunately, Lindsey wasn't away from home for too long. After making it into the Top 12, which was a remarkable accomplishment for any performer, she was voted off the show during the first week of the finals. "I really had a wonderful time in Los Angeles. I've met a lot of new friends here. I'm not so upset about being voted off the show. What I am upset about is that I won't be able to spend time with all of the new friends I've made here," added Lindsey, who realizes that her experience on *American Idol* was only the beginning of what she hopes will be a long career in the music business.

Behind-the-Scenes Moments

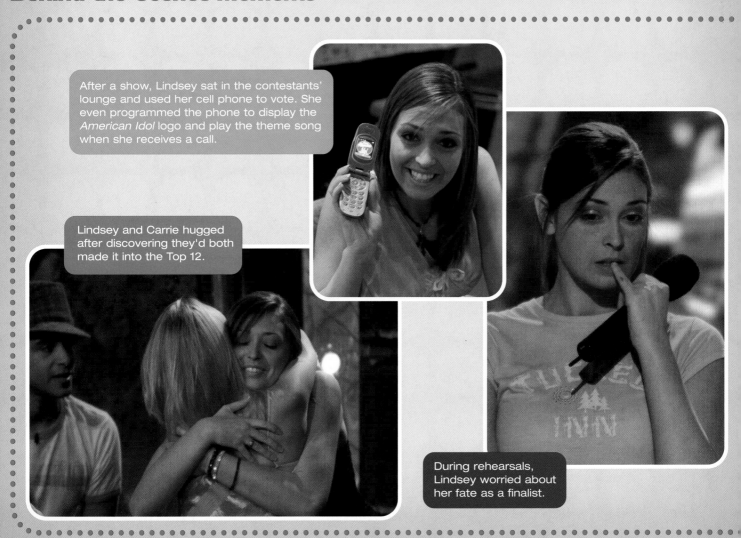

After a show, Lindsey sat in the contestants' lounge and used her cell phone to vote. She even programmed the phone to display the *American Idol* logo and play the theme song when she receives a call.

Lindsey and Carrie hugged after discovering they'd both made it into the Top 12.

During rehearsals, Lindsey worried about her fate as a finalist.

Ever since the Top 12 were selected, all the finalists were competing for just one spot as the winner of the competition. "I don't know what America is looking for in terms of their next American Idol. At the time, all I could do was my very best work and hope that people watching the show enjoyed my performances," said Lindsey. She also wishes she had more time on the show in order to showcase her talents singing other genres of music.

When you look at the Top 12, it's easy to see why some of the finalists made it, while others were sent packing. Lindsey believes that one reason why she made it into the Top 12 was because of her ability to add a lot of emotion into the songs she performs. "I am a strong person who can add emotion to my music, but at the same time successfully deal with the many emotions we feel as a result of being a contestant on this show," said Lindsey.

For Lindsey, being a Top 12 finalist was a dream come true.

Lindsey had plenty of fans in the audience during the first week of the Top 12 competition.

Lindsey and Carrie became close friends during the competition.

Here's Lindsey rehearsing with *American Idol*'s vocal coach, Debrah Byrd.

Millions of *American Idol* fans saw Lindsey progress through the auditions and into the Top 12, during which time we got to know a bit about her from watching the show. "The biggest misconception people have about me is that I'm a quiet and shy person. That's not the case at all. When I am nervous, I get quiet. Typically, I am a very outgoing person," she explained. "I'm sorry people watching the show didn't get to see that from me."

Even after she was voted off the show, Lindsey was grappling with the reasons why she was invited into the Top 12 to begin with. "At the auditions, there were so many really amazingly talented people. I saw people being sent home at the New Orleans auditions and then in Hollywood whom I thought had as much or more singing talent than me. I don't exactly know what the judges and producers saw in me, but I am grateful for the faith they had in me and my talent. I was honored to be part of this year's competition," she concluded.

Performance Highlights

Lindsey had a chance to shine during the semi-finals.

She was the first to go during the finals this season on *American Idol*, but Lindsey won't soon be forgotten.

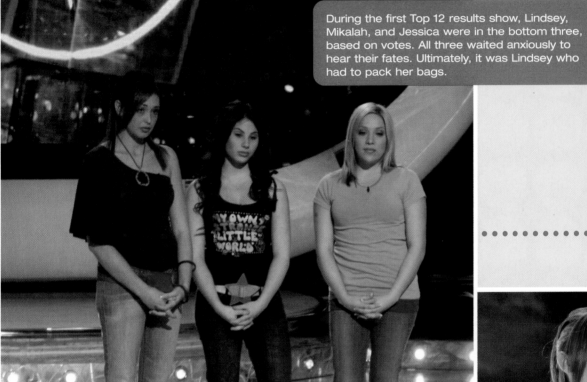

During the first Top 12 results show, Lindsey, Mikalah, and Jessica were in the bottom three, based on votes. All three waited anxiously to hear their fates. Ultimately, it was Lindsey who had to pack her bags.

Lindsey offered a heartfelt farewell performance of "Knock On Wood" after Ryan told her she'd been voted off the show.

Lindsey brought a touch of country music to the *American Idol* stage.

MIKALAH GORDON

The Inside Scoop

As the youngest performer in this season's Top 12, Mikalah can best be described as having the personality and talent of comedian Fran Dresher (The Nanny) combined with award-winning recording artist and actress Barbara Streisand. Week to week, it's been impossible to predict what to expect when Mikalah takes center stage, because as a performer, she's willing to take risks and try many different genres of music.

"I love surprises and I am a surprising person. I think the last thing on people's minds after seeing me during the first few weeks on the show was that I could perform a ballad and do it well. During the last week of semi-finals, I wanted to show audiences a different side of me. I was very pleased with how it turned out," explained Mikalah, who often uses humor to deal with her nervousness.

"
People really like me or they don't. It's a love/hate thing.
"

Idol Fast Facts

Hometown................................Las Vegas, NV
Audition City...........................Las Vegas, NV
Birthday................................January 14, 1988
Sign...Capricorn

ON THE PERSONAL SIDE...

Favorite Recording Artists:	Barbara Streisand, Bette Midler, Donna Summer, and Aretha Franklin
Favorite Food:	Pasta
Favorite Color:	Leopard
Favorite TV Show:	*Rocko's Modern Life*
Favorite Movie:	*Dumb and Dumber*
Favorite Subject in School:	Lunch
Worst Subject in School:	Math
Pets:	"I have a younger brother named Sam, but no pets."
Hobbies:	Hip-hop dancing and singing

Seventeen-year-old Mikalah is currently a high school junior. Appearing on *American Idol*, however, hasn't meant having a school vacation. Everyday, she spends at least three hours with a private tutor and must keep up with all of her school work, in addition to juggling the demands put on her by the show. She explained, "One minute I'm on the stage belting out my favorite song. The next minute, I am working with a tutor studying history and vocabulary."

When she's in school back in Las Vegas, Mikalah is a cheerleader and participates in choir and the theater club. While she's been in Hollywood working on *American Idol*, one of her projects has been finding a high school prom date.

Back in Las Vegas, as a part-time job, Mikalah also worked at the New York-New York Hotel & Casino at an oxygen bar. "I worked there for a year. Visiting an oxygen bar gives you a boost of energy and wakes you up," she explained.

When asked to describe herself, Mikalah stated, "I think I am very fun and boisterous. I'm a warm person. There's also a very deep side to me. In a word, I'm fabulous!"

Early in her life, Mikalah decided she wanted to be a singer and performer. When *American Idol* held auditions in her hometown, she couldn't resist attending. "The whole audition experience was a bit nerve-racking. The day of the auditions, if you were to ask me if I'd be making it into the Top 12, I would have said absolutely not. There were so many very talented people who tried out, but didn't make it. When I made it to Hollywood, Simon Cowell complimented me when he said I was the most confident 16-year-old he's ever met. This whole experience has been a tremendous learning experience. When I found out I made it into the Top 24 and then the Top 12, I absolutely flipped out," said Mikalah.

When she was packing to come to Las Vegas, Mikalah packed her baby blanket, which she calls "Jenny." She brings it everywhere. *American Idol*'s producers require a parent to be with the under-age contestants every step of the way. Because Mikalah is a minor (under age 18), her mother, Victoria, has been traveling and staying with her while she's been in Los Angeles.

"I really miss my dad, brother, and sister, along with my friends from back home. I'm trying to follow my dreams. This is well worth everything I've been through," said Mikalah, who dreads the Wednesday night results shows.

Behind-the-Scenes Moments

During the semi-finals, Mikalah showed a more serious and sophisticated side to her talent.

During a lunch break, Mikalah called one of her friends.

Mikalah works hard with vocal coach Debra Byrd, associate music director John Beasley, and music supervisor Susan Slamer to choose her songs and create customized arrangements during rehearsals.

"Sometimes, having talent and giving 100 percent just isn't enough to stay in this competition. I've seen a bunch of very talented people get voted off the show already, plus I was in the bottom three in terms of votes during the first week of the Top 12 finals. That was very stressful. During the results shows, when I'm sitting on the couch waiting for Ryan to tell us the results, I keep thinking about everything I could have done differently or better," said Mikalah, who is proud of her accomplishments thus far and knows in her heart that she's put everything she has into each of her performances.

In the past, Mikalah has studied voice with a private teacher. She also sang once at The White House for former President Clinton. "I performed as part of a holiday show. It was a very memorable and fun experience," she recalled.

Ryan and Mikalah chatted after one of her semi-final performances.

Vocal coach Debra Byrd and Mikalah chatted in the Red Room prior to a semi-finals show.

During the semi-finals, Jasmine Trias from Season 3 dropped in for a visit. Mikalah enjoyed meeting the former finalist.

During the early weeks of the finals, in an attempt to stay in the competition, Mikalah began focusing on the music, as opposed to showing off her personality. "I will continue to take risks and do things that people don't expect, but my focus is now entirely on the music. People should know that I am a crazy person with a crazy sense of style. The way I dress is based on how I feel on a particular day. Sometimes, I like to dress like a private school girl and sometimes I like to dress like a punk," she said.

Everyone has seen Mikalah's outrageous side. She wants people to know, however, that she's also kind, loving, and can be very serious. "That's who I am. I don't want people to underestimate me just because I'm only 17," she added. "Every time I step on the *American Idol* stage, I perform for myself, for God, and for the audience. For that short time I am performing, I am giving the performance everything I have. People really like me or they don't. It's a love/hate thing."

Performance Highlights

The audience saw the emotional side of Mikalah. At this time, she was in the bottom three, based on votes during the results show after the first week of the Top 12 finals competition.

When Mikalah takes to the stage, audiences seldom know what to expect.

In the weeks she's spent in Los Angeles working on *American Idol*, Mikalah admits she's learned more in this short time than she has during her entire life prior to this experience.

"There have been a lot of ups and downs, but overall, this as been an incredible experience which I wouldn't trade for anything in the world. I now have a tremendous amount of respect for everyone who has ever stepped onto the *American Idol* stage and attempted this. This is definitely not as easy as it looks on television. The most important lesson I've learned thus far is to trust my own instincts," she concluded.

When she performed a power ballad, Mikalah showcased her more serious side. While her personality is more like comedian Fran Dresher, from a singing standpoint, could Mikalah be a young Barbara Streisand in the making?

Seventeen-year-old Mikalah was often praised by the judges for taking risks with her song selections, but criticized for choosing songs that were "too old for her."

While some may find her annoying, others find Mikalah lovable and talented

Mikalah and the rest of the Top 12 finalists rehearse their first group production number on the *American Idol* stage.

NADIA TURNER

The Inside Scoop

At age 28, Nadia is an accomplished fashion model and singer. To supplement her income, however, she also works as a bartender. The *American Idol* finalist credits her mother for helping her to pursue her dreams of becoming a recording artist. "If anyone has been the most supportive throughout my life, it's definitely my mother," explained Nadia, who was also on bowling, soccer, and track teams in high school. These days, to keep her ultra-trim figure, Nadia enjoys swimming and roller skating.

Aside from becoming a Top 12 finalist on *American Idol*, another highlight in Nadia's life was when she traveled to Japan in 2002, to perform for the President of the United States and a handful of other world leaders and delegates. "Eight world leaders got together for a summit and I was hired to perform for them. President Clinton complimented me on how good my voice is. That experience was beyond incredible," recalled Nadia, who landed the gig performing for the President after auditioning for an international record label.

"

When the judges told me I'd made it into the Top 24, at first I thought they were joking.

"

Idol Fast Facts

Hometown:..Miami, FL
Audition City: ....San Francisco, CA
Birthday:.............................January 11, 1977
Sign: ....Capricorn

ON THE PERSONAL SIDE...

Favorite Recording Artists:	**Prince, Outkast, Jimi Hendrix, Billy Joel, and the Eagles**
Favorite Food:	**Spareribs**
Favorite Color:	**Blue**
Favorite TV Show:	*The Golden Girls*
Favorite Movie:	*Forrest Gump*
Favorite Subject in School:	**English**
Worst Subject in School:	**Math**
Pets:	**A turtle named "Moe" and a cat named "Mellow"**
Hobbies:	**Black and white photography and attending wine tastings**

Several years ago, when Nadia was working at an upscale restaurant, the manager required the staff to become extremely familiar with wine. Nadia began attending wine tastings and developed an appreciation for fine wines from around the world.

Nadia enjous her time in America and abroad. Growing up, she spent almost every summer of her life vacationing in Saint Eustatius. "It's the most beautiful place I've ever visited. My mother is Dutch and a lot of our family lives there. Some of my fondest memories from childhood took place when I was visiting Saint Eustatius with my family," she explained.

"I would describe myself as eccentric. I am a positive and fun person to be around. I'm also a spiritual person. Everything I have done has been through God's will," explained Nadia, who admits she almost didn't audition for *American Idol* and never really watched the show during previous seasons.

She explained, "My best friend is a doctor in New York. She put our friendship on the line and said that if I didn't audition for the show, she'd never speak to me again. She also offered to cancel appointments with her patients so she could fly out to San Francisco with me to attend the auditions. My friend thought I was perfect for the show. I kept putting off going to the auditions until the very last city the producers visited, which was San Francisco. Now, whenever I speak with my friend, all she has to say is, 'I told you so!'"

If you've watched Season 4 of *American Idol*, you already know that Nadia is all about making fashion statements with what she wears and how she styles her hair. She seldom, however, wears dresses. "I'm a jeans type of person. When I packed to come to Los Angeles, I brought along all of my favorite jeans and T-shirts, because that's what I enjoy wearing and what I'm most comfortable in. I also packed one of my grandmother's dresses and my Bible," said Nadia.

"My taste in fashion and style comes from what I like. I don't read the fashion magazines or anything. I just wear what I think looks good. I am flattered to know that people are vibing my style. I'm not trying to set any fashion trends, but if someone likes what I wear and wants to copy it, they should run with it. I love fashion, but I don't have a lot of money to buy fancy designer outfits, so I always make do with what I can afford. In the past, I've done some modeling for fashions shows," added Nadia, who has been missing her family while she's been in Los Angeles competing on *American Idol*.

Behind-the-Scenes Moments

Looking as glamorous as ever, Nadia enjoyed the attention she received on the red carpet as she entered the FOX party and celebrated making it into the Top 12.

Nadia is all about being stylish.

After making it into the Top 12, reporters from across American wanted to chat with Nadia, including *Entertainment Tonight*.

It took over an hour in the hair and make-up room to create Nadia's ultra-stylish mohawk look.

Nadia feels totally comfortable performing on stage and isn't bothered by *American Idol*'s studio audience or the TV cameras. What sometimes stresses her out, however, is being judged by Simon, Paula, and Randy when she performs. "I know that not everyone will like everything I do. My strategy as I participate in this competition is to avoid trying to be someone I'm not. I know I can sing, but I won't ever perform a song that isn't suitable for my voice or style. I am not Mariah Carey or Whitney Houston," she said.

Just moments before Nadia steps on stage to perform, she always eats an Altoids mint and says a prayer. "After I made it past the first round of auditions, I was invited to Hollywood. Never before had I been surrounded by so many talented people. When the judges told me I'd made it into the Top 24, at first I thought they were joking," recalled Nadia.

Now that she's made it into the Top 12 and has proven she has what it takes to potentially win the competition, what Nadia dislikes most about participating in *American Idol* are the Wednesday night results shows. "We spend so much time with our fellow finalists that when someone leaves our group and is voted

Nadia experiments with a new hairstyle during a rehearsal.

Nadia and Anwar look like fashion models as they pose for a photo backstage, just before a show.

From the Red Room, Nadia watched her fellow contestants perform.

Her previous modeling experience helped to prepare Nadia for the hours she'd spend in hair and make-up getting ready for each show.

off the show, it's really tough emotionally. I've bonded with several people on the show who I know I will stay in touch with regardless of what happens to us during the competition," added Nadia, who enjoys taking bubble baths to help her relax and relieve some of the stress associated with the show.

To win this competition, Nadia believes the key is to be herself, work hard, and to focus on her uniqueness. "As a result of making it into the Top 12, I believe my life will change dramatically from this point forward. What I've learned about myself thus far is the importance of having some quiet time or down time periodically to help me stay focused," concluded Nadia, who really appreciates the support she's received from her countless fans.

Performance Highlights

When Nadia sings, it's with total conviction and dedication!

Nadia's powerful voice wows television viewers on a weekly basis.

She sang "Time After Time," but it was the first time Nadia showed off this hot-looking mohawk hairstyle.

Fans can expect big things from Nadia. In the words of Paula, "You look like a star. You look like a rocker."

You can see the determination in Nadia's eyes every time she steps on stage.

You can always count on Nadia to look hot, but sound hotter!

NIKKO SMITH

The Inside Scoop

"Before *American Idol*, I was a struggling artist," explained 23-year-old Osborne Smith II, who is now known to millions of television viewers as "Nikko." During the third week of the show's semi-finals, Nikko was voted off the show, despite the fact that many people believed he was extremely talented and deserved to make it into the Top 12.

After being voted off on Wednesday, Nikko returned home to St. Louis the following night. On Friday, at around 2:30 AM, he was awakened by a phone call from one of the show's producers who informed him that he'd be replacing Mario in the Top 12 and that he needed to be back on an airplane at 7:30 AM in order to immediately begin rehearsing back in Los Angeles.

> " I've always got to rock the hats. "

Idol Fast Facts

Hometown: ....St. Louis, MO
Audition City:.........................St. Louis, MO
Birthday:................................April 28, 1982
Sign: ....Taurus

ON THE PERSONAL SIDE...

Favorite Recording Artists:	**Marvin Gaye, R. Kelly, Rascal Flatts, Jodeci, and Dru Hill**
Favorite Food:	**Chicken**
Favorite Color:	**Royal Blue**
Favorite TV Shows:	***Tom & Jerry, Dragon Ball Z,* and *Law & Order***
Favorite Movie:	***Good Will Hunting***
Favorite Subject in School:	**"Did I have one of those? Probably science."**
Worst Subject in School:	**Math**
Pets:	**A dog named "Scrappy"**
Hobbies:	**Playing video games**

This was an incredibly lucky break for Nikko, who was thrilled to have a second chance at showcasing his musical abilities to America. "It feels really good to be back at *American Idol* as part of the Top 12. I'm sorry about the circumstances, however. I didn't want anyone to leave the competition. Being back is really good," said Nikko, who didn't even have time to unpack at home in St. Louis before he was asked to return to Los Angeles.

During his short time at home between getting voted off the show and the first week of Top 12 competition, Nikko spent a few hours hanging out with his friends and had dinner at his favorite fast food restaurant, Chick-fil-A. He admits he's not sure why he was voted off the show, but upon his return, Nikko vowed to work even harder at staying in the competition.

The first week he was in the Top 12, Nikko performed the classic Jackson 5 song, "I Want You Back," in honor of his unexpected return to the competition. Growing up, Nikko was no stranger to being in the public eye. His father is the well-known former Major League Baseball player, Ozzie Smith. However, Nikko admits he's not at all a sports fan.

"My father tried to offer me some advice on how to deal with fame and prepare for my experience on *American Idol*. However, I don't think there's really anything anyone can do to fully prepare for this experience," said Nikko. "The biggest misconception people have about me is that they think I am here on this show because of my dad. The reality is, he had absolutely nothing to do with me making it onto *American Idol*. I went to the auditions like everyone else and earned my spot here just like everyone else."

Now that Nikko is in the Top 12, he believes people watching the show at home don't realize just how challenging it is to perform on the *American Idol* stage and to be a finalist in the competition. "Choosing the right songs and then going up on stage knowing that tens of millions of people are watching is very scary. Each time we step on stage, we have less than two minutes to show people what we can do and to give them a really good show," he said. "I try to choose songs that feel good to me and that most people will know."

One thing that sets Nikko apart from the other finalists is his unique sense of style, which he describes as "hip-hop meets intellectual, with a touch of class." He added, "I've always got to rock the hats. The fedora hat is my trademark thing. I try to be pretty stylish. When I wear one of the fedora hats, I am paying tribute to performers from the 1960s and the Rat Pack."

Behind-the-Scenes Moments

Here's Nikko rehearsing in the contestants' lounge.

Looking ever so dapper, Nikko sat in the Red Room waiting to perform during the semi-finals.

During week three of the semi-finals, Nikko stood on stage with Travis and Scott as Ryan Seacrest revealed that Nikko and Travis were voted off the show. Less than three days later, however, the producers invited Nikko back into the competition. It was a lucky break for Nikko!

Nikko showed off his fashionable belt that has a built-in LCD display that scrolls animated text messages.

Nikko believes the hardest part about being a contestant on *American Idol* is choosing the perfect song and then creating a customized arrangement for it. "A typical song lasts three to five minutes. On *American Idol*, we only have between 90 seconds and two minutes to perform each week. We have to make sure that our song arrangements are really good. Cutting down and editing songs is a huge challenge," said Nikko, who believes he's become a lot more focused since he first auditioned for the show.

After being voted off the show during the semi-finals, Nikko discovered firsthand just how important hard work is in order to stay in the competition. "Everyone who has made it this far in the competition is absolutely amazing in terms of their talent. If we're not totally focused at this point, we'll be voted off the show," he said.

After returning as a Top 12 contestant, Nikko immediately began rehearsals with Michael Orland and Dorian Holly. Executive producer Nigel Lythgoe sat in on this particular rehearsal as well.

Top 12 finalists Anwar, Nikko, and Constantine relaxed on the Red Room set right before a dress rehearsal for a semi-finals show.

You can almost always catch Nikko wearing one of his trademark hats. He wears them to pay tribute to his favorite performers from the past, including the Rat Pack.

Whenever Nikko steps onto the *American Idol* stage to perform, he refuses to think about the high stakes. Instead, he focuses on the in-studio audience and on the television cameras in order to insure he offers the best performance possible. "Who becomes the next *American Idol* is totally up to America. All I can do is keep doing what I've been doing and keep trying to give really good performances. I consider myself to be a versatile performer, which I think will help me a lot in the competition, especially during the theme shows," explained Nikko, who has made some very close friends with other finalists on the show.

"I guess this is a competition against other performers, who are also my friends, but I don't look at it like that. The only person I am competing against is myself. If I get up there and do what I do to the best of my ability, and I offer a better performance than I did the previous week, I've done exactly what I'm supposed to do," he said.

Nikko describes himself as a laid-back and cool cat, who is also a homebody.

Performance Highlights

The performance outfit Nikko chose made him look as stylish as ever.

During his first performance as a member of the Top 12, Nikko offered up an impressive performance on the new *American Idol* stage. He demonstrated that he totally deserved to be back!

Like all of the finalists, Nikko knows the importance of putting a ton of emotion and feeling into the songs he performs.

Even without a hat, Nikko proved he had the right look and an amazing voice as he performed during week 2 of the semi-finals.

SCOTT SAVOL

The Inside Scoop

When a contestant becomes a finalist on *American Idol*, one perk, if you want to call it that, is that they receive a security detail when they go out in public. After all, the *American Idol* contestants have quickly become some of the most popular celebrities in Hollywood. Scott, however, doesn't necessarily need his own security. Prior to landing his spot in the Top 12, he worked as a private security guard while helping to raise his four-year-old son.

"Spending time with my son is probably the thing I enjoy most in life. When I'm not working or with my son, you can typically find me in church," explained the single, 28-year-old father and *American Idol* finalist.

"

I'm hoping people will look beyond my appearance and focus on my vocal skill and personality.

"

Idol Fast Facts

Hometown.............................Cleveland, OH
Audition City.........................Cleveland, OH
Birthday.................................April 30, 1976
Sign...Taurus

ON THE PERSONAL SIDE...

Favorite Recording Artists:	Fred Hammond, Luther Vandros, Usher, Michael Bolten, and Alicia Keys
Favorite Food:	His mom's homemade lasagna
Favorite Color:	Blue
Favorite TV Show:	*The Jamie Foxx Show*
Favorite Movie:	*What Dreams May Come*
Favorite Subject in School:	Math
Worst Subject in School:	Criminal Justice
Pets:	A dog named "Maggie"
Hobbies:	Drawing, songwriting, and surfing on the net

"I think I am different from most people. I grew up in a predominately African-American neighborhood. I don't really identify with people based on their skin color or ethnic background. I can get along with pretty much everyone. I am not an aggressive or tough person," he added. "I like to smile, laugh, and have a good time. I don't think *American Idol* viewers have had a chance to really see that side of me. I am really a fun-loving guy who is very laid back."

Scott has wanted to audition for *American Idol* every year since Season 1, but, at first he was too old. When the producers raised the age limit to 28, Scott was finally able to audition. "I found out they changed the age requirements about three days before the actual auditions. I took the day off from work and went to see what it was all about," recalled Scott, whose previous singing experience was primarily in conjunction with his church. He's also performed at a few festivals and events in the Cleveland area.

The first time Scott showed up to audition for *American Idol*, the judges almost dismissed him because of his appearance. After he started singing, however, the judges changed their tune and quickly invited him to Hollywood.

"When I traveled to the Hollywood auditions, it was my first trip ever to the west coast, so that was exciting. I met a lot of different people from across America, so it was a wonderful experience. On television, people didn't see me portrayed in the best possible light during the audition episodes. The group part of the audition process didn't go so well for me. My group members didn't want to take full advantage of our rehearsal time, so we had some personality clashes early on. I was then portrayed as the bad guy on TV. Ultimately, it all worked out for the best. I take my music seriously, so when we were given a chance to rehearse, I wanted to take full advantage of every minute available to us," said Scott, who was truly humbled to become part of the Top 12.

Upon coming to Los Angeles to compete in the semi-finals, Scott packed a handful of photos of his son, a good luck pin from his cousin, and some of his favorite music to listen to when he has time to relax.

Behind-the-Scenes Moments

Sometimes, the schedule for the finalists gets so busy, they need to take a midday nap in the contestants' lounge in order to keep up their energy.

Here, Scott goes over some song ideas with Michael Orland, *American Idol*'s associate music director.

During a rehearsal, Scott kicked back on the plush red leather couch in the Red Room.

"I also brought my Bible to help me keep my mind focused. There are passages in the Bible that comfort me and give me peace of mind," explained Scott, who believes that his life revolves around his relationship with God.

The further Scott makes it in the competition, the harder he feels he needs to work each week. "It's not about just singing to the audience. When I perform, I need to connect with the audience on an emotional level. Each week, I need to step up my performances and that's really challenging to do," added Scott. "Being able to hit the right notes is important, but what makes a great singer is someone who can make you feel something strong when you hear them perform."

Scott works hard during all of his rehearsals, but he's also learned the importance of making the most of what little free time he has. "When we have some time to relax, I utilize it to the fullest. I know it's important to stay rested and to take care of myself. I think that the winner of *American Idol* this season will have to be unique and have the type of voice that people haven't heard before. When people look at me, they never expect me to sing the way I do. I'm hoping people will look beyond my appearance and focus on my vocal skill and personality," said Scott.

Scott and Lindsey took a break for lunch and dined in their dressing rooms.

After being told the following week's theme would be songs from the 1990s, Scott pondered over a list of popular songs from that decade.

Scott spends countless hours each week rehearsing for every performance.

Scott and executive producer Ken Warwick chatted about the new *American Idol* sets during a camera blocking rehearsal.

Performance Highlights

Scott isn't about wearing fancy clothes.... He's all about being an everyday guy who believes in God and who wants to be known as someone who always does his very best.

Like every contestant, Scott is relieved and grateful when he discovers he's been voted through to another week.

Scott often wears a metal dog tag that is imprinted with a photo of him and his young son.

"Against All Odds" was the song Scott chose to perform during week two of the Top 12 finals. He dedicated the performance to his dad.

Scott is a fun-loving and upbeat guy, but he takes his music very seriously.

Scott may not look like your typical *American Idol*, but each time he performs, he proves he has exactly what it takes vocally to be in the Top 12.

VONZELL SOLOMON

The Inside Scoop

She goes by the nickname "Baby V," but during the second week of the Top 12 final rounds of competition, Vonzell Solomon celebrated her 21st birthday on the *American Idol* set. Her fellow finalists gave her the new nickname "Lady V" in honor of her becoming a legal adult.

During this birthday, Vonzell had a lot to celebrate. In recent weeks, she had gone from being a full-time mail carrier in her hometown of Ft. Myers to becoming a Top 12 finalist on America's most popular television show.

> In terms of my style, I am who I am.

Idol Fast Facts

Hometown:..............................Ft. Myers, FL
Audition City: ....Orlando, FL
Birthday:...........................March 18, 1984
Sign:..Pieces

ON THE PERSONAL SIDE...

Favorite Recording Artists:	**Destiny's Child and Aretha Franklin**
Favorite Food:	**Spaghetti and meat balls**
Favorite Color:	**Pink**
Favorite TV Show:	**"I don't watch too much TV."**
Favorite Movie:	***Willy Wonka and the Chocolate Factory***
Favorite Subject in School:	**Language Arts**
Worst Subject in School:	**Chemistry**
Pets:	**A dog named "Buster." He's a pit bull.**
Hobbies:	**Martial arts, collecting anything with Minnie Mouse on it, writing poems, and listening to music**

In addition to being a singer, Vonzell is also an athlete. In high school, she played basketball and soft ball, plus she's been studying martial arts since she was five. She's currently a third-degree black belt. "I can break boards and bricks, but I've never had to use my fighting skills outside of the dojo," explained Vonzell, who originally auditioned for Season 2 of *American Idol*, but didn't make it past the first phases of auditions.

Vonzell was so determined and confident in her singing abilities, she returned to the Season 4 auditions and managed to thoroughly impress the producers and judges. "I attended a high school for the performing arts and studied music for four years. I also sing at church and at private parties. I would describe myself as fun-loving, funny, and a bright person who loves to smile," she said.

Prior to auditioning for *American Idol*, Vonzell recorded a full-length demo CD, which she was using to help her get the attention of record label executives. "The CD I recorded featured original R & B, hip-hop, and soul music that I wrote," added Vonzell, who hopes to have little trouble landing a recording contract once she's done with *American Idol*.

Vonzell is enjoying her time in Los Angeles working on the show. What she misses most about home, however, are the home-cooked meals her mother prepares. "I miss my family a lot. I also miss being able to drive my own car and listen to my loud music when I drive," explained Vonzell, who, like many of the finalists, continues to find choosing the right songs to perform on *American Idol* one of the biggest challenges she faces each week.

"My strategy for selecting songs is simple. I find songs I really feel. I also rely on my family for advice. In terms of my style, I am who I am. I hope America continues to accept me just for being me. My goal is to come across on TV as I really am. I never want people to be afraid to approach me or speak to me. I love meeting new people," said Vonzell.

"At home, a lot of people know me because I'm from a pretty small city. It totally amazes me that I am now in Los Angeles and when I go out in public here, total strangers come up to me, know who I am, and ask for my autograph," stated Vonzell, who is doing her best to live in the moment and enjoy every minute she spends working on *American Idol*.

Behind-the-Scenes Moments

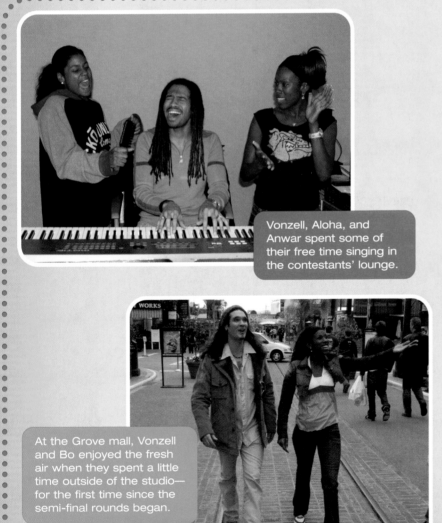

Vonzell, Aloha, and Anwar spent some of their free time singing in the contestants' lounge.

At the Grove mall, Vonzell and Bo enjoyed the fresh air when they spent a little time outside of the studio—for the first time since the semi-final rounds began.

Vonzell looked totally at home on the red carpet as she posed for photographers. The following morning, she said her face hurt from smiling so much.

To deal with the pressure and stress associated with being a Top 12 finalist, Vonzell relies on meditation and prayer. One of the few personal items she brought with her to Hollywood, aside from clothes to wear on the show, was her bible. She added, "I think it's my faith in God that has allowed me to hold it together throughout this competition. Having studied martial arts for so many years has also helped me. It taught me self discipline and patience."

Despite all of the challenges the finalists face, Vonzell knows that to succeed, she'll need to be original and be herself. "I know that every time I step onto that stage, I have to give 210 percent. That means I have to pour my heart and soul into every single performance. My strategy is simply. I try to stay true to myself. I plan to work extremely hard for as long as I'm in this competition," said Vonzell.

Two stylists work on Vonzell's hair prior to the first Top 12 competition show. Within a few short hours, she emerges from the hair and make-up room with a totally new and beautiful look.

Vonzell is a third-degree black belt and has studied martial arts for most of her life.

Producer Simon Lythgoe went over some important show details with Vonzell.

Since coming to Hollywood, Vonzell's life has changed a lot. "I think my life will be fabulous after this experience, even if and when I wind up getting voted off the show. As a result of appearing on *American Idol* and making it into the Top 12, I know many doors will be open for me after this is over. This is a great opportunity which is very exciting," added Vonzell, who is a firm believer in pursuing her dreams and working very hard to make them a reality.

After spending several weeks in the Top 12, Vonzell has begun to feel comfortable performing for millions of TV viewers. She admits that she's been a huge fan of the show since Season 1 and really respects what Fantasia and other past winners have accomplished. "Fantasia's CD is fantastic. I could listen to it all day, every day. I also love Kelly Clarkson, but I relate more to Fantasia because she sings the type of music I really enjoy performing," concluded Vonzell.

Performance Highlights

Vonzell looks beautiful and sophisticated in the long pink dress she wore for the first Top 12 competition show of the season.

Attitude, emotion, and passion are just some of the ingredients Vonzell mixes together as she performs on the *American Idol* stage.

Vonzell showed off a touch of country when she dressed in denim and a cowgirl hat for one of her semi-final performances.

Each week, Vonzell has managed to muster up not just an impressive performance but a new look as well. No matter what she's wearing, however, she always looks stylish and classy.

She may be soft-spoken, but when she's on stage and the song requires it, Vonzell can belt out those powerful notes just like a true professional.

Throughout the *American Idol* season, each of the Top 12 finalists embark on an amazing journey that transforms them from being singers into true performers capable of becoming superstars in the music industry. This transformation is made possible thanks to a team of extremely talented people whom you never actually see on television, yet each one plays an extremely important role in the contestants' lives and in making *American Idol* the #1 rated show in America.

The Making of an *American Idol*:
The Transformation Begins

For each show, it takes literally several hundred people, all working behind the scenes throughout the entire week, to get *American Idol* on the air. You're about to meet just a handful of the people who are directly involved with the contestants, making them look and sound their absolute best.

Simon Fuller
Creator and Executive Producer

Nigel Lythgoe and Ken Warwick
Executive Producers

As the executive producers, Nigel Lythgoe and Ken Warwick oversee every aspect of *American Idol*'s production. They're in charge! They're also the creative forces behind the show.

Simon Fuller and judge Simon Cowell have a great working relationship.

Simon Fuller is the guy who created *American Idol* as well as 30 other versions of the show that currently air throughout the world. He's also the president of 19 Entertainment, a successful talent management and TV production company that represents several of the world's most popular recording artists, including a handful of past and present *American Idol* finalists and winners.

Simon and Nigel enjoy a quick reunion with Season 3 runner-up Diana DeGarmo at a party.

When the contestants are rehearsing in the contestants' lounge, Ken often drops in to watch and offer his support.

The two producers work closely with Susan Slamer, *American Idol*'s music supervisor.

During the Season 4 semi-finals, Jasmine Trias from Season 3 dropped by the set to say hello. Nigel and the rest of the crew were glad to see her.

Cecile Frot-Coutaz
Executive Producer

Ken and Nigel handle the day-to-day creative decisions and the production of *American Idol*, while executive producer Cecile Frot-Coutaz handles more of the business-related issues pertaining to the show. Cecile is the Chief Operating Officer for FremantleMedia North America, Inc. (FMNA), a division of global television producer FremantleMedia. Along with overseeing a lot of the business and operational matters pertaining to *American Idol*, she is responsible for overseeing current productions and managing all business and financial aspects of the company's production slate.

Wylleen May
Executive in Charge of Production

As the Executive in Charge of Production, Wylleen May manages the show's budget, hires and coordinates the large production crew, and makes sure that everything the producers need is available to them. She oversees many of the logistics involved with getting America's most popular show on the air.

Meet the Producers

It's the job of the producers not just to manage the day-to-day schedules of the contestants, but to shoot and produce all of the pre-taped segments, called "packages," that you see on the show.

During the *American Idol* season, these producers work six to seven days per week, up to 18 hours per day. They're often on the job at least two hours before the contestants even wake up in the morning. While the hours are long, the producers are the first to admit how much they love their job and how much fun it is to work on such a popular television show.

A handful of producers work on *American Idol*, but it's Patrick Lynn, Megan Michaels, and Simon Lythgoe who work most closely with the contestants from the very start of the audition process through the season finale.

Megan Michaels
Producer

Megan works with all the contestants throughout the season and is one of the producers who visits finalists' hometowns to film interviews with the their friends and family members. Megan also plays an important role at all of the auditions; she's one of the producers for whom contestants initially audition, before they get to audition for the executive producers and, ultimately, the judges.

Patrick Lynn
Coordinating Producer

Patrick's job is to help coordinate what the other producers do and implement the creative ideas of the executive producers. He's also in charge of overseeing the contestants' schedules and supervising the production of the pre-taped segments you see on the show.

Simon Lythgoe
Producer

Working closely with the executive producers, along with Patrick and Megan, Simon is also heavily involved in the audition phase of the competition. As the season continues, his job focuses more on managing the contestants and shooting the pre-taped segments you see on the show.

FremantleMedia

With 260 different shows currently airing in 39 countries, FremantleMedia is one of the largest international creators and producers of television programming in the world. Responsible for bringing *American Idol* to more than 30 countries across the globe and adapting the show into new formats like *Canadian Idol*, *Indonesian Idol*, and *Malaysian Idol*, aspiring Idols from every corner of the Earth have a chance to be a star.

In the U.S., FremantleMedia and its team of producers work with 19 Entertainment and FOX to produce every episode of *American Idol*, making sure that they deliver the most entertaining talent show ever created to millions of viewers each week.

As the licensing arm for *American Idol*, FremantleMedia is the reason fans can pick up the latest *American Idol* magazine, stay connected with their pals through *American Idol* Instant Messaging, style out with new T-shirts, collect awesome trading cards, play with the newest *American Idol* Barbie doll, and enjoy a plethora of other fun things. The company also works with FOX to maintain the idolonfox.com website, which continues to be one of the most popular destinations on the Web with approximately one billion visitors during the season.

FremantleMedia is always looking for cool new ways to experience *American Idol*, so be on the lookout for the latest gear and technologies featuring America's most watched television show.

19 Entertainment

As one of the leading talent management companies in the world, 19 Entertainment, in tandem with Freemantle Media, works with all *American Idol* semi-finalists and finalists during the entire *American Idol* season and throughout the *American Idol* Live Tour, which the company produces.

After the tour, the management company selects a few of the most talented finalists, including the winner and often the runner-up, to work with on an ongoing basis. Getting picked up by 19 Entertainment after *American Idol* is one of the first major steps finalists take to becoming successful recording artists.

19 Entertainment works closely with the show's producers and, ultimately, the record label to help transform the finalists into chart-topping recording artists, launch their careers, and then manage them as they ultimately release their solo albums and tour.

Throughout the season, several talent managers and representatives from 19 Entertainment can always be found on the set looking out for the finalists' best interests and helping to manage their hectic schedules.

The Music Team

Helping the vocalists sound incredible is the job of *American Idol*'s music team. These professionals have worked with some of the biggest names in the music business and are responsible for countless chart-topping hits.

Rickey Minor is the *American Idol* band leader and helps to create the musical arrangements for every song the contestants perform. Season 4 is Rickey's first *American Idol* season.

Rickey Minor
Music Director

When it comes to music and the recording industry, Rickey Minor plays a major role. This talented bass player not only leads the *American Idol* band, he's also a successful music producer, arranger, and composer, as well as a television producer.

Over the years, Rickey has worked with Whitney Houston, Usher, Destiny's Child, Britney Spears, Ray Charles, Stevie Wonder, Elton John, Rod Stewart, NSYNC, and Alicia Keys, just to name a few.

Each of the semi-finalists and Top 12 finalists during Season 4 got to jam with Rickey Minor and the *American Idol* band every time they performed.

Susan Slamer
Music Supervisor

Susan is directly involved in helping each contestant select the songs they per-

form on the show, although she's quick to confirm that each contestant must choose his or her own song selection for every performance. She works closely with the show's associate music directors and vocal coaches, including Dorian Holly, Debra Byrd, Michael Orland, and John Beasley.

When there's a theme show, such as "disco week," "big band," or "movie themes," it's often Susan who helps choose the theme and who invites the guest judges or recording artists to appear on the show.

Susan hung out in the contestants' lounge with the all the Top 24 guys just moments before they stepped on stage to perform during round one of the semi-finals.

Once song selections are made, Susan obtains permission for the contestants to sing the songs from the various recording artists, songwriters, and music publishing companies.

At a party, Susan had a mini-reunion with Season 3 Top 12 finalist Jon Peter Lewis and heard all about the new album he's working on.

For Season 4, Byrd works primarily with the female semi-finalists and finalists, including Mikalah Gordon. Her job is to help each contestant develop and protect their voices, plus improve their vocal performances from week to week.

Debra Byrd
Vocal Coach (Females)

Having worked on all four seasons of *American Idol* and several seasons of *Canadian Idol*, Debra Byrd, whose nickname is "Byrd" on the set, has worked with all the former Top 12 finalists from seasons past.

Aside from her work on this show, Byrd is a highly accomplished singer, vocal coach, and music arranger. For the past 20 years, she's been working closely with Barry Manilow as his music arranger and backup singer. Most recently, she helped Manilow create his Las Vegas show, *Manilow: Music and Passion*. Schedule permitting, she also appears in his show as a guest performer.

Throughout the week, Byrd and associate music director John Beasley spend the most time in rehearsals with each of the female contestants, such as Carrie Underwood.

When the *Today* show visited the set of *American Idol*, host Katie Couric interviewed Byrd, along with the judges and Ryan Seacrest.

John Beasley
Associate Music Director (Females)

Working closely with Byrd and the female semi-finalists and finalists during Season 4 of *American Idol*, John's job is similar to Michael Orland's.

Joining the production team of *American Idol* this season is composer and pianist John Beasley. On the show, John works closely with vocal coach Debra Byrd to help prepare each of the female contestants for their performances on the show.

Prior to working on *American Idol*, John worked with dozens of well-known recording artists, like Chaka Khan, Miles Davis, Al Jarreau, Johnny Lang, Ricky Martin, Kelly Clarkson, Queen Latifah,

Barbara Streisand, Fantasia, Cheryl Crow, Destiny's Child, Gloria Estafan, Bette Midler, and Bonnie Raitt.

John has also written and performed the music used in dozens of motion pictures and television shows, including: *Finding Nemo, Hope Floats, The Godfather III, A Bug's Life, Fried Green Tomatoes, Austin Powers: The Spy Who Shagged Me, Happy Days, Star Trek: The Next Generation, Fame, Family Ties*, and *The Division*.

John, Byrd, and Ken help Lindsey Cardinale and all the female contestants create their personalized song arrangements and then rehearse for their performances.

Dorian works with all the male semi-finalists and finalists on *American Idol*, and has the same responsibilities as Byrd. This, however, is his first season working on America's most popular talent competition.

Dorian Holly
Vocal Coach (Males)

During his 18 years working in the music industry, Dorian has worked as a backup singer and vocal coach to literally dozens of famous artists, including Michael Jackson, James Taylor, Rod Stewart, Fantasia, Usher, and Stevie Wonder. Dorian is also a teacher of R & B vocal performance at the Los Angeles Music Academy and is currently putting the final touches on his own album. It's no wonder why *American Idol*'s producers recruited him to work with the male contestants on the show this year.

Dorian works closely with Michael Orland, the show's associate music director.

This season on *American Idol*, Michael works with the guys to help them develop their song arrangements and rehearses with them throughout each week. Here, Michael is working with Nikko just hours after Nikko replaced Mario in the Top 12.

Michael Orland
Associate Music Director (Males)

Michael has been playing piano and keyboards for much of his life. Prior to getting involved with *American Idol* during Season 2, he worked with some of Broadway's biggest performers and other popular recording artists as a musician, vocal coach, songwriter, and music arranger.

It's All About the Look

Being a good singer isn't enough to win the *American Idol* competition or to become a pop superstar. Personality and looks play a huge role in any artist's success. Some of the people who help the finalists fine-tune their look for TV include the hairstylists, make-up artists, fashion consultant, and choreographer.

Throughout the season, these experts spend countless hours with each of the Top 12 finalists.

Dean Banowitz "The Hollywood Hair Guy"
Lead Hairstylist

As the lead hairstylist on the show, Dean is responsible for making sure Ryan Seacrest's hair always looks perfect. During the Top 12 phase of the competition, Dean and his team also work with each of the remaining contestants.

When a contestant reveals their new look on the show, it was typically created by Dean and his team of hairstylists.

Dean has been involved with *American Idol* since the start of Season 1 and is partly responsible for the visual transformations of the contestants. Before each show, he typically spends between 20 minutes and one hour with each finalist.

Mezhgan Hussainy
Lead Make-Up Artist

Hair and make-up play crucial roles in helping all of the *American Idol* finalists look their absolute best. As the show's lead make-up artist, Mezhgan works on all the Top 12 finalists, Ryan Seacrest, Simon Cowell, and Randy Jackson, helping to make their skin look natural, yet flawless on camera.

Miles Siggines
Lead Fashion Consultant

As *American Idol*'s fashion consultant, Miles helps Ryan Seacrest and the Top 12 finalists choose what to wear each week on the show. Not only does Miles ensure that the contestants keep up on the latest fashion trends, he also helps to create them.

Carrie Ann Inaba
Choreographer

Carrie Ann Inaba and her assistant choreographer, Mandy Moore, are responsible for creating the dance moves featured in all of the group production numbers seen on *American Idol* every Wednesday night.

As the show's choreographer, Carrie Ann and Mandy create the dance steps that go along with the group performances, then teaches them to the finalists. Much of thier work involves teaching the Top 12 finalists how to move on stage.

During the Top 12 phase of the competition, the results shows on Wednesday nights usually feature a choreographed group performance by all the remaining finalists. It's Carrie Ann Inaba and Mandy Moore who puts the group performances together.

The Rest of the Team

Producing any television series offers a tremendous number of challenges. Working on a television show that airs live several times per week and that stars an ensemble of previously untrained talent (as opposed to professional actors or entertainers) is probably the toughest job in show business.

Hundreds of people on the crew, who are the best in the business, help to make the production of *American Idol* appear effortless.

Award-winning director Bruce Gowers works in the studio's master control room and tells the camera crews what to shoot in order to ensure that viewers always get to see the best shots of the performers.

During the live shows, stage manager Debbie Williams calls the shots and tells everyone on stage exactly what to do.

Corey, the show's audience warm-up guy, entertains the in-studio audience before every show begins. He also introduces the judges, Ryan, and the contestants when they take their places moments before show time.

Keeping the judges, Ryan, and all the contestants safe is the job of Michael Boschetti and his highly trained security team.

You see the main stage and Red Room sets each week on *American Idol*. Now, here's a behind-the-scenes peek at television's most popular stage and a look at where the contestants spend most of their time when they're working throughout the week to prepare for each show.

American Idol Sets:
A Look Backstage and Behind the Scenes

Just before the semi-final rounds begin, the main *American Idol* sets, which include the stage (surrounded by a small audience) and the Red Room, were built. It took a large team working around the clock to build the *American Idol* sets in time for the first live broadcast. After the basic set was built, hundreds of lights plus a state-of-the-art sound system were installed.

Behind these giant doors is stage 36 at CBS Television Center in Hollywood. Inside this building is the home of *American Idol.*

Does it look familiar? This would soon become the *American Idol* stage and judges' deck for the semi-final rounds of the competition.

For Season 4, *American Idol* began broadcasting in high-definition television. This meant that all-new equipment needed to be installed in the studio's master control room. With more than a dozen cameras shooting every show, the master control room is an extremely busy place during the live broadcasts.

Thanks to the hard work of dozens of talented people, the *American Idol* set began to take shape.

This year, the Red Room set featured brand-new, bright-red leather couches that were custom-made for the show.

As the main stage was being built, the adjoining Red Room set was also constructed.

Check out this view. This is what the contestants saw when they were standing on the main stage looking out into the audience and TV cameras while they performed.

While the finishing touches were being made to the sets, the contestants began rehearsing on the main stage. Soon, close to 30 million people would be watching them perform on this very stage.

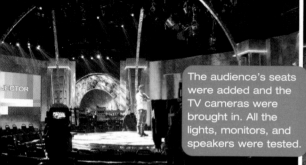

The audience's seats were added and the TV cameras were brought in. All the lights, monitors, and speakers were tested.

When the sets were built and the lights were turned on, the *American Idol* stage looked amazing.

On the second floor and down this hall was where all the contestants' dressing rooms were. During the semifinals, two or three contestants shared each dressing room, however, it was common for people to hang out in the hallway.

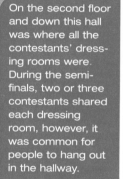

Directly behind the *American Idol* sets was the "green room." This living room-like area was where the contestants could relax right before the show. *Green room* is a show-biz term. The room wasn't really green.

The third floor of the studio contained two large rooms that were the contestants' lounges. Here, the semifinalists spent many hours rehearsing with one of the show's associate music directors and vocal coaches.

In the contestants' lounge, there was plenty of room to rehearse choreography in front of the giant mirror. There was also plenty of room in the contestants' lounge to kick back and relax. That is, when they weren't rehearsing.

The new Red Room set was painted, new carpeting was installed, and the couches were brought in. Soon, the room took on a very familiar look.

All-New Sets Are Built for the Finals

Within minutes after the third semi-final results show aired, the Red Room set and main set were totally dismantled and stage 36 was cleared out.

In just four days, all-new sets had to be built. To accommodate the much bigger stage, the new Red Room set was built in one of the third floor contestants' lounges, instead of on stage 36.

The Top 12 finalists checked out the new Red Room set.

It took another huge team to transform the giant empty soundstage into what would soon be the new *American Idol* set. The set designer created this model to help the crew visualize what the final set would look like.

After the new Red Room set was built, back on sound stage 36, construction began on the massive new, state-of-the-art main set. This year, the set has a whole new look. It's bigger and fancier than ever before. Within 24 hours, the giant empty soundstage started to resemble what would soon be the main *American Idol* set.

As the massive construction effort got underway, pieces of the new set were built elsewhere and brought to the soundstage in huge trucks.

The giant screen on the main stage looked amazing!

Piece by piece, the set came together. The clock was ticking, however. In this picture, the first live show to be broadcast from this set was less than 48 hours away.

Executive producer Nigel Lythgoe checked out the new set and was very impressed.

Soon, more than 450 seats would be installed here, where the studio audience would sit.

The *American Idol* set looked incredible when it was finished. All the finalists were in awe the first time they stepped foot on the stage.

Constantine and the rest of the finalists quickly made themselves at home on the new stage as they offered up awesome performances throughout the final rounds of competition.

In just 11 weeks from when the first Top 12 competition show aired, *American Idol* would move to the Kodak Theater in Hollywood for the star-studded, two-night season finale.

Just in time for the first live show, the set was completed and the audience took their seats.

A Taste of Stardom

Just a few weeks after discovering they'd made it into the Top 24, the remaining contestants were flown back to Hollywood to participate in the competition's semi-final rounds. After checking in at their Beverly Hills hotel, preparations for the first live shows immediately began.

For the first week of semi-finals, each Top 24 contestant had less than two minutes to perform one song, impress the judges, and showcase their talent to over 30 million television viewers. During each emotionally charged results show, the two guys and two girls who received the fewest votes were immediately sent home. The schedule was grueling and the competition was intense.

The American Idol 4 Semi-Final Rounds

The Semi-Finals: Day One

When the contestants arrived at the studio in the morning, their first task was to choose the song they'd be performing.

Each contestant had a chance to meet with American Idol's vocal coach and pianist to create the customized arrangement for their song selection. After that, they spent the rest of the day rehearsing on their own. They had just three days to prepare before performing for the millions of TV viewers who would ultimately decide their fate.

American Idol's music supervisor Susan Slamer worked with each contestant to help them select the songs they sang throughout the season. Ultimately, it was up to each contestant, however, to choose the songs they sung. In this competition, song selection is critical! Check out Susan hanging out with the Top 12 guys in one of the contestant lounges.

About halfway through the day, executive producers Nigel Lythgoe and Ken Warwick gathered everyone in the third floor contestants' lounge for an important meeting. During this gathering, the contestants got all of their questions answered.

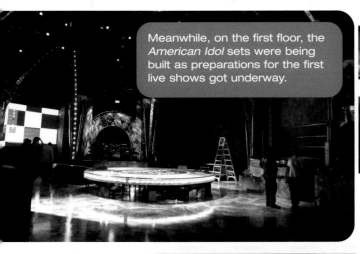

Meanwhile, on the first floor, the *American Idol* sets were being built as preparations for the first live shows got underway.

For the first time, *American Idol* would be broadcast in high-definition television, which meant installing a lot of new equipment on the set and in the master control room. During Season 4, the show would be seen in more than 30 countries throughout the world, although only American viewers could vote.

During a break, a few of the guys got together in the contestants' lounge to try their luck playing the *American Idol* board game...as if experiencing the real thing wasn't enough.

Some of the contestants decided to play Twister within one of the more cramped dressing rooms in between their rehearsals.

The Semi-Finals: Day Two

As the girls began the song selection process in preparation for Tuesday's competition show, the guys had a full day of rehearsals. Each person had about one hour to meet with the vocal coach and pianist. The rest of their day was spent rehearsing on their own.

At the end of a long day, some of the contestants relaxed by gathering around a keyboard and singing TV-show theme songs. Anwar Robinson played the keyboard as most of the Top 24 contestants participated in the sing-along.

Joe Murena received dance lessons from Amanda Avila and Lindsey Cardinale.

Scott Savol, Anthony Fedorov, and Jared Yates surfed on the www.idolsonfox.com website to check out what fans were saying online about them. Jared checked out the candid Polaroid photos he and his fellow contestants posted on the photo board.

SEASON 4 109

The Semi-Finals: Day Three

For the guys, this was their first chance to rehearse with the band on the main *American Idol* stage. The guys immediately made themselves at home on stage as each of them offered up a stellar performance during rehearsals.

Anthony Fedorov was one of the first guys to rehearse on the *American Idol* set. Like all the guys, he quickly made himself comfortable on the stage and offered a performance that was nearly flawless. He demonstrated exactly how he beat out more than 100,000 other *American Idol* hopefuls to reach this point in the competition.

Each of the Top 24 contestants performed with Rickey Minor and the *American Idol* band. Check out this talented group of musicians and backup singers as they worked with each contestant.

Judd Harris showed off his energetic personality as he rehearsed for his performance of "Travelin' Band." During rehearsals, the contestants use water bottles instead of microphones.

During each rehearsal, Dorian Holly, the guy's vocal coach, along with associate music director Michael Orland and executive producers Nigel Lythgoe and Ken Warwick, offered advice as each performance was fine-tuned. Although he is a music teacher himself, Anwar Robinson paid careful attention to the criticism and instruction he was offered.

Mario Vazquez and David Brown put a ton of emotion and energy into their rehearsals as well.

Meanwhile, in the third floor contestants' lounge, the girls experienced their second day of rehearsals as they continued to master their song arrangements while working with vocal coach Debra Byrd and associate music director John Beasley.

The Semi-Finals: Day Four

The guys had a free day today as they each rehearsed on their own, plus caught up on some much needed sleep. Meanwhile, the girls woke up bright and early to experience their first day rehearsing on the *American Idol* stage with the band.

Byrd worked with Janay and all the female contestants individually to perfect their on-stage performances.

Executive producer Nigel Lythgoe shared his thoughts about Jessica Sierra's first rehearsal on the *American Idol* stage with Byrd and the girls' associate music director John Beasley.

Even during rehearsals, Nadia Turner showed she could belt out "Power of Love" with an incredible amount of emotion and power.

Aloha Mischeaux received words of encouragement from Byrd as she stepped on stage to rehearse "Work It Out." When performance time came, that's exactly what she ultimately did!

Amanda Avila rehearses on the *American Idol* stage for the very first time.

Vonzell Solomon loved working with the live band as she rehearsed "Heatwave."

One by one, each of the female contestants took center stage and rehearsed in front of the producers, Byrd, John Beasley, their fellow contestants, and a handful of people from *American Idol*'s crew.

The Semi-Finals: Day Five

After several days of intense rehearsals, it was show time! The guys were picked up at their hotel at 8:00 AM. Once they got to the studio, they participated in a camera blocking rehearsal.

This rehearsal offers the director, stage manager, camera crew, and sound technicians the chance to plan out the show while the contestants rehearsed on stage with the band. It was followed by a full dress rehearsal and then the actual show.

Before the show, associate music director, Michael Orland, and Dorian Holly, the guy's vocal coach, met backstage to discuss the upcoming performances and to make their predictions.

Producer Megan Michaels offered the finalists some last minute advice and direction before their performances.

Just after noon, everybody took a much-needed lunch break. The contestants had about one hour to eat, get dressed for the show, style their hair, and be back on stage for a full dress rehearsal.

Jared Yates and Ryan Seacrest chatted on the main stage during the dress rehearsal.

Just before the dress rehearsal, Ryan Seacrest hung out on the Red Room set with the Top 12 guys.

At 20 minutes before showtime, the contestants returned to the set. They had all anxiously watched the dress rehearsal from the Red Room set when they weren't performing.

While the studio audience took their seats and the live band started to warm up, Ryan Seacrest worked with the producers to make last-minute changes to the show's script.

During the dress rehearsal, the cameras were rolling, host Ryan Seacrest was on the set, and everything was exactly like the actual show. This was the final chance for each semi-finalist to rehearse on stage. The only differences between the dress rehearsal and the actual show are that the judges don't attend the dress rehearsal and there's no studio audience.

Immediately after the dress rehearsal, the guys returned to the contestants' lounge. They had about 30 minutes to relax, rehearse on their own, or make last minute adjustments to their wardrobe. At this point in the competition, the semi-finalists received no advice or help from the show's hairstylist, make-up artists, or fashion consultants.

Just before the first show of the semi-finals, judge Paula Abdul made a surprise visit to the contestants' lounge. She presented each of the guys with a special "good luck" gift—a bracelet from her personal jewelry line called Innergy. Each bracelet had the inscription, "When you wish upon a star, you might just become one." The following night, the Top 12 girls received similar gifts from the former pop princess.

The First *American Idol* Season 4 Semi-Final Round

It was on Monday night's show that the guys performed on the *American Idol* stage, while the Top 12 female semi-finalists watched from the audience. These mostly impressive performances were a preview of what viewers could expect from the rest of the season.

Kicked Off with a Bang!

Check out the view from judge Simon Cowell's seat at the judge's table.

After their performances, each contestant took turns facing the judges.

Up first, Nikko Smith performed "Part Time Lover." He was followed by Scott Savol, who offered up his rendition of "You Are My Lady."

The power ballads kept coming as Anthony Fedorov performed an amazing rendition of "Hold On to the Night." He looked excited and confident just moments before he stepped onto the American Idol stage.

Rock-and-roller Constantine Maroulis sang "Kiss from A Rose." It was then David Brown's turn to take the stage with his rendition of "Never Can Say Goodbye."

Eighteen-year-old Jared Yates performed a wonderful rendition of "How Could I," but unfortunately failed to impress the judges with his song selection. The performance, however, was one he could be proud of.

As the show continued, it became incredibly clear that this was going to be an amazing season. Bo Bice added his rock-and-roll flare to "Drift Away" and had the audience clapping, while the girls in the audience swooned over Travis Tucker's performance of "My Cherie Amour."

Anwar Robinson proved why he was invited into the Top 24 when he performed "Moon River."

According to the judges, their favorite performance of the night came from Mario Vazquez, who ended the show on a high note with "Do I Do."

Judd Harris picked up the pace and showed a few dance moves when he sang "Travelin' Band," which was followed by Joe Murena singing "How Am I Supposed to Live Without You."

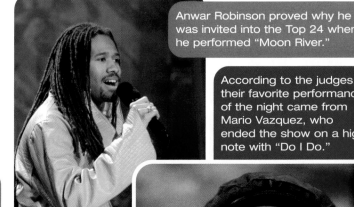

With the performances over, the guys had to wait until Wednesday night to learn how America voted. Two of the Top 12 guys would soon be headed home.

The Semi-Finals: Day Six

As Tuesday night rolled around, it was the girls' turn to show off their talent for America. The female semi-finalists proved that talent, personality, and beauty are qualities they each possess.

Things got really hot on stage when Vonzell Solomon kicked off the night's performances with "Heatwave." Taking a more mellow route, Amanda Avila performed "How Am I Supposed To Live Without You."

As the youngest girl in the competition, Janay Castine proved she could compete with the older semi-finalists as she sang "I Wanna Love You Forever." During this first performance, however, she appeared very nervous. Just before stepping on stage, Janay had a problem with her contact lenses, so she removed them. So, although we could see her on TV, she had a hard time seeing much of anything.

Melinda Lira sang "Power of Love." She was followed by an amazing performance by Nadia Turner, who showed off her unique style, attitude, and beauty as she too belted out "Power of Love."

Millions of guys watching at home were immediately captivated by Carrie Underwood's beauty and charming personality as she stepped onto the American Idol stage to sing "Could've Been." Up next was Sarah Mather, who picked up the tempo a bit with her rendition of "Get Ready." Unfortunately, in this case, it was Sarah who needed to get ready—to go home.

Celena Rae received positive criticism from the judges after she sang "I Will Love Again." Mikalah Gordon proved that her outgoing personality isn't the only thing she has going for her. When she sang "Young Hearts Run Free," she showed off her unique singing style. Even if she failed to receive enough votes to stay on the show, Mikalah was determined to convince judge Simon Cowell to be her high school prom date.

Lindsey Cardinale performed "Standing Right Next to Me," which Jessica Sierra followed by singing a heart-felt rendition of "Against All Odds." Jessica dedicated her performance to her mother, who passed away during the American Idol audition process, just weeks before Jessica came to Hollywood.

Tuesday night's semi-finals competition show ended with Aloha Mischeaux singing "Work It Out," which is exactly what she did on stage with her impressive and attitude-filled performance.

A very lucky Ryan Seacrest ended the show with a group hug from the girls.

Could one of these Top 12 female semi-finalists become the next *American Idol*? Or, will it be one of the guys who ultimately wins the competition?

The Semi-Finals: Day Seven

The finalists put in many hours of rehearsals this week. Now, each contestant was ready to see if their hard work paid off. This evening, during the live results show, Ryan revealed who would stay in the competition and who would be among the first to be sent home. It was a highly-charged, merciless, and emotional hour of television. Many believed this was *American Idol*'s harshest results show ever.

After the show, those who made it were extremely excited, but the four finalists who were voted off were understandably very upset. Plenty of tears flowed.

Nobody knew what to expect as the drama of the season's first results show unfolded on live television.

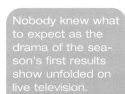

The female semi-finalists were invited on stage first as Ryan created a full hour's worth of anticipation and drama before revealing all the voting results from Monday's and Tuesday's competition shows.

Everyone was very nervous about the first results show of the season.

The pressure was on! Who would stay? Who would go?

Next, it was the guys' turn to take their seats on the bleachers as Ryan told America which of the male semi-finalists would be leaving the competition after receiving the least votes. They all looked petrified during the commercial break before Ryan shared the results.

Melinda Lira was the first of the Top 24 finalists to discover she'd been voted off the show when Ryan shared the shocking news with America.

Sarah Mather also discovered her participation in the *American Idol* competition was coming to a sudden end.

Jared Yates was the youngest of the Top 12 guys and, unfortunately, the first to be voted off the show. His charm, teen heartthrob looks, and Marc Anthony-like voice would definitely be missed.

During the final moments of the first results show of the *American Idol* 4 season, it was Judd Harris who learned that he, too, would be leaving the competition. He offered a wonderful farewell performance before the show ended.

Imagine the uncertainty and pressure Anthony and the other contestants experienced during this incredibly stressful live results show.

After the first results show, the remaining 10 girls and 10 guys posed for photos.

In the contestants' lounge, as he was waiting for the show to begin, Bo took a short nap and had happy dreams of becoming the next *American Idol*.

Mirror, mirror, on the wall, who's the hottest semi-finalist of them all?

Jessica said goodbye to Judd after the show.

The Semi-Finals Continue...

The morning after the results show, the 20 remaining contestants arrived at the studio to begin preparations for week two of the semi-finals. Once again, they'd select a song to perform, spend several days rehearsing, and then perform live.

Each week for three weeks, two more guys and two more girls would be voted off the show. By the end of week three, over 120 million votes would be cast by viewers and only 12 contestants—six guys and six girls—would remain as the competition really heated up.

After the first week of semi-finals, only 20 contestants out of 100,000 remained in the competition. Over the next 14 weeks, 19 of these talented people would also be eliminated, leaving just one *American Idol* winner.

The Results Are In

It was on three consecutive Wednesday night shows that Ryan Seacrest managed to keep TV viewers and the contestants anxiously waiting for him to reveal the results of each week's voting.

By the end of the three semi-final rounds, for half of the Top 24, their *American Idol* journey was at an end. The contestants performed. The judges offered their comments. America voted. The votes were counted. Here's who got eliminated during the semi-final rounds:

SEMI-FINALS
Week 1 Eliminations
Wednesday, February 23, 2005

Melinda Lira

Jared Yates

Sarah Mather

Judd Harris

SEMI-FINALS
Week 2 Eliminations
Wednesday, March 2, 2005

David Brown

Joe Murena

Aloha Mischeaux

Celina Batchelor

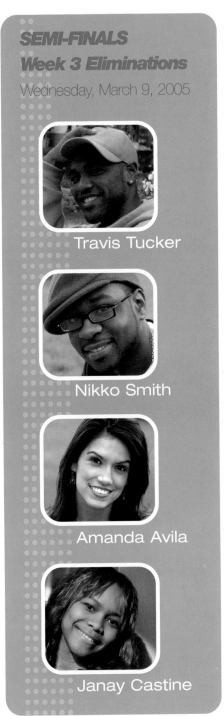

SEMI-FINALS
Week 3 Eliminations
Wednesday, March 9, 2005

Travis Tucker

Nikko Smith

Amanda Avila

Janay Castine

During three months of finals, when the competition goes from the Top 12 contestants down to just one winner, the week-to-week *American Idol* production schedule is extremely hectic.

As you'll soon discover, everyone works seven days a week, and long days of hard work are the norm. For the finalists, each new round of competition begins on Wednesday. As the weeks progress, the stakes are higher and the pressure intensifies.

In this section, you'll follow the finalists through a typically hectic week as they prepare for the live shows.

The Contestants' Weekly Schedule

Wednesday

Wednesday is the day the finalists dread! An emotionally draining day, Ryan reveals who's been voted off during the live show. For the finalists, though, a lot must happen before the live broadcast.

7:00 AM: Rise and Shine

A typical Wednesday begins at 7:00 AM, when the contestants wake up. By 8:30 AM, they must be on set, ready to rehearse the group production number with choreographer Carrie Ann Inaba. There's no sleeping late when you're competing on this show!

8:30 AM to 10:30 AM: Time To Rehearse the Group Production Number

The finalists have two hours to put the finishing touches on the group production number. Not only do they need to rehearse their singing with Debra Byrd and the *American Idol* band, they must also master the choreography.

In just a few hours, the finalists need to learn new choreography for the group production number, then rehearse it until it looks perfect.

Not all of the *American Idol* finalists can dance. This poses a challenge for choreographers Carrie Ann Inaba and Mandy Moore, who must make all of them look equally good on stage as they perform.

While many of the finalists dread Wednesdays because of the emotional rollercoaster they'll experience during the results show, they all love performing together during the group numbers.

3:00 PM: Report to Hair and Make-Up

Due to the three hour time difference between the east coast and west coast, *American Idol* goes on the air live at 6:00 PM (California time). Starting at 3:00 PM, the finalists report to the hair and make-up department to start preparing for the night's show. The mood is typically a bit stressful since in just a short time someone will be packing their bags and headed home.

The good news for the finalists is that they'll reunite over the summer when they embark on the *American Idol* Live nationwide tour. They'll also perform together again during the *American Idol* season finale on May 24th and 25th.

5:30 PM: Gather in the Green Room

About 30 minutes before showtime, the finalists gather in the green room, which is located behind the main *American Idol* set. The audio department gives each contestant their clip-on microphone, then everyone waits for the show to begin. Five minutes before airtime, the finalists are escorted onto the main stage.

Starting at about 5:15 P.M., the studio audience takes their seats.

6:00 PM: The Live Results Show Airs

At exactly 6:00 PM, Ryan Seacrest takes center stage and the process of revealing the week's voting results kicks off. Everyone who watches the show knows that Ryan uses every minute of the show to build suspense.

The lights dim and the finalists line up on stage for the opening camera shot. In showbiz lingo, it's called a "Cold Open."

Near the start of the results show, the remaining finalists perform a group production number. This season, viewers voted on which group number was released on CD and to radio to raise money for the American Red Cross.

Usually, early in the results show, Ryan reveals that at least a few of the finalists are "safe" and will be staying in the competition. He'll then often invite the contestants with the fewest votes to take center stage. The drama and suspense build up fast, yet Ryan always manages to go to a commercial just before revealing anything.

After the commercials and stalling tactics, the voting results are finally announced. One person is sent home each week. During that person's final moments on stage, they watch a short retrospective video created by the producers, then have a chance to sing one last time before packing their bags.

The person voted off the show sings a farewell song. Their *American Idol* journey and quest for superstardom has come to a disappointing end.

7:00 PM: Remaining Finalists Meet in the Red Room

Immediately after each results show, Ryan and the remaining finalists meet up in the Red Room on the third floor. During this meeting, the finalists are told what the theme of the following week's show will be.

The remaining finalists always participate in a photo shoot on the Red Room set after the results shows. Meanwhile, the person who was voted off starts packing.

Once the contestants know the show's theme for the following week, they'll have about 24 hours to select the song they want to perform the following Tuesday. It's a lot to think about, considering that rehearsals begin first thing on Thursday morning.

7:45 PM: Meeting with Susan Slamer

After the finalists discover the next week's theme, *American Idol*'s music supervisor, Susan Slamer, meets with everyone to review a long list of potential songs.

Ultimately, each contestant must choose for themselves what song they'll sing, but Susan always offers up a list of several hundred suggestions.

Susan gives a selection of appropriate songs to the contestants and plays a sampling of music that is suitable for the week's theme.

Each week, Susan and the producers choose a theme for the show, such as music from the 1960s, 1970s, 1980s, or 1990s, disco, big band, country, Billboard #1 hits, or movie themes. Before rehearsals begin on Thursday morning, each finalist must pick their song selection.

9:30 PM to 11:00 PM: The Farewell Dinner

To honor the person who was voted off the show, and to give the finalists a chance to say goodbye, the producers host a weekly farewell dinner.

Thursday

8:00 AM: Rehearsal Begins

During this first day of the week's rehearsals, the remaining female contestants meet with vocal coach Debra Byrd and associate music director John Beasley, one at a time in the third floor contestant's lounge. Meanwhile, each of the guys work with vocal coach Dorian Holly and associate music director Michael Orland.

The farewell dinners are typically upbeat and fun, yet sad at the same time. After all, one of the finalists will be headed home in the morning.

If the contestant already knows what song they will sing, they get to work creating the personalized arrangement for that song. Otherwise, the vocal coach and associate music director help kick around ideas with the finalist as they make their song selection.

This first rehearsal is typically when the three- to five-minute song is cut down to the 90-second to two-minute version that the finalist will actually perform on the show.

After a multi-course meal that is attended by all the remaining contestants, friends, family members, and several of the show's producers, the finalists return home to get a good night's sleep. Starting at 5:00 AM the following morning, the person who is leaving the show will do several hours worth of live TV and radio interviews before heading home.

One at a time, each finalist gets about an hour of rehearsal time with the vocal coach and associate music director. The rest of the day, the contestants can hang out in their dressing rooms and rehearse on their own.

Friday

It's another busy day of rehearsals at the *American Idol* studios. During their one-on-one rehearsal sessions, the finalists use this valuable time with the vocal coach and associate music director to nail down exactly how they'll perform their song selection. The producers and Susan Slamer often sit in on these rehearsals.

9:00 AM to 6:00 PM: Rehearse, Rehearse, Rehearse…and Shop!

Once again, these rehearsals take place in the two contestants' lounges on the third floor. After a finalist knows what song they will be singing, they need to set a time to go shopping for wardrobe with Miles Siggins, *American Idol*'s fashion consultant. For each Tuesday's performance show, the finalists need a new outfit to wear. They're given a weekly budget to go shopping.

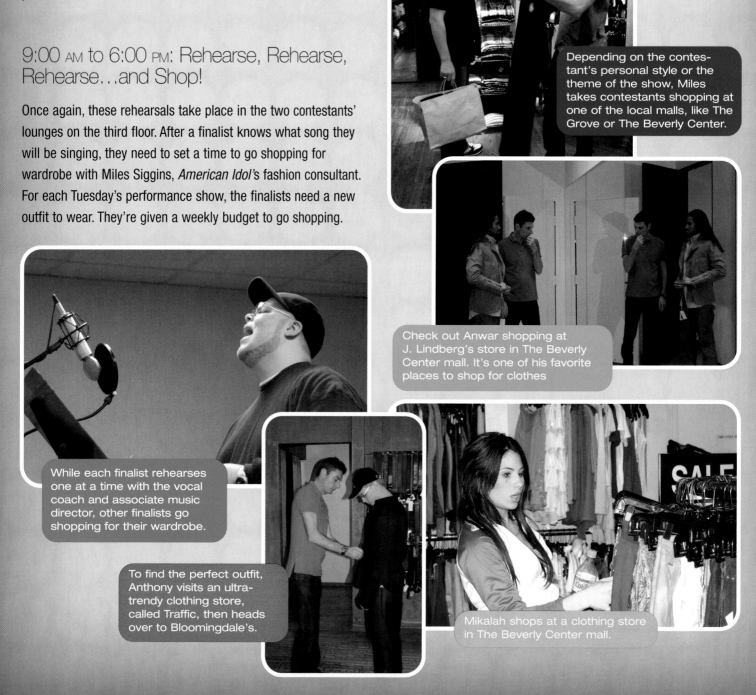

Depending on the contestant's personal style or the theme of the show, Miles takes contestants shopping at one of the local malls, like The Grove or The Beverly Center.

Check out Anwar shopping at J. Lindberg's store in The Beverly Center mall. It's one of his favorite places to shop for clothes

While each finalist rehearses one at a time with the vocal coach and associate music director, other finalists go shopping for their wardrobe.

To find the perfect outfit, Anthony visits an ultra-trendy clothing store, called Traffic, then heads over to Bloomingdale's.

Mikalah shops at a clothing store in The Beverly Center mall.

Anwar loves trendy clothing with a retro twist. He often finds clothes on Melrose Avenue in Hollywood, at a store called Wasteland

Carrie starts off by window shopping at The Grove as she searches for an outfit to wear on the show.

Saturday

9:00 AM to 5:00 PM:
Rehearsals with the *American Idol* Band

Yes, the *American Idol* finalists work throughout the weekend. On Saturday morning, they show up to the set and begin rehearsing with the full band. It's during this rehearsal they also work out any choreography they'll use during their performances. They rehearse on the actual *American Idol* stage, instead of in the contestant's lounge.

The Saturday rehearsals on stage are pretty casual.

As each finalist rehearses, the other finalists watch from the audience and offer each other support and constructive criticism.

One at a time, each remaining finalist rehearses their song. The producers, vocal coaches, associate music directors, and band all watch and participate.

It's during this rehearsal that the finalists can experiment with different ideas regarding their performance.

Sunday

8:00 AM to 6:00 PM: Shoot the Ford Music Video

Every week, *American Idol* features a "Ford Moment," which is an original music video the remaining finalists spend all of Sunday shooting. The music video's producers (who are different from the *American Idol* producers) choose a song, then quickly develop a concept for a fully-produced music video that will air on Wednesday night's results show.

Before a single frame of footage can be shot, the finalists need to record the audio soundtrack for their music video at a recording studio in Hollywood. This process alone takes several hours.

Shooting a music video can take anywhere from 8 to 15 hours of hard work. By the end of the day, the finalists are exhausted but satisfied.

Each video is shot on location, usually somewhere in Hollywood or Los Angeles.

For each "Ford Moment" video, you can expect the finalists to sing and dance. Keep your eye out, however, for one of Ford's newest cars to make cameo appearances throughout the video.

While the music videos are usually a lot of fun to shoot, sometimes the finalists have to shoot the same footage 5, 10, or even 20 times in a row. Phew!

Monday

9:00 AM to 12:00 PM: Group Production Number Rehearsal

On Monday morning, vocal coach Debra Byrd starts working with the remaining finalists on the group song they'll perform live during Wednesday night's results show. During this rehearsal period, the group must learn a new song, plus rehearse the production number.

The finalists gather in one of the contestants' lounges and begin rehearsing the group production number. Each finalist's vocal skills are taken into account when the group song is selected.

1:30 PM to 3:30 PM: Rehearse Choreography

After the finalists start getting to know the lyrics for the group song they'll perform, they meet up with choreographers Carrie Ann Inaba and Mandy Moore to start learning the dance moves that accompany the song.

Carrie Ann and Mandy create original choreography for every group production number. The dance moves she choreographs need to look amazing on TV, but be easy enough for everyone to learn in a very short time.

Some of the finalists are incredible dancers, while others have two left feet. Sometimes, Carrie Ann or Mandy need to work extra hard getting some of the contestants up to speed so they look good performing the dance moves on stage.

Tuesday

9:00 AM: It's Show Day!

By now, the finalists should have their song memorized and be ready to perform live on stage in front of millions of television viewers (and the judges, of course).

One of the first things the contestants do on Tuesday morning is to participate in a walk-through and camera blocking rehearsal for that night's show. This takes two to three hours.

Head stage manager Debbie Healy, the producers, camera crew, and show director Bruce Gowers go through every minute of the upcoming show, tell Ryan and the contestants where they need to be, and help the camera crew choose their best shots.

For each live *American Idol* show, there are more than a dozen TV cameras on the set to catch every second of the action. Each camera must shoot the right thing at the right time to make the show look fantastic when it goes on the air.

12:30 PM to 2:30 PM: The Hair and Make-Up Process Begins

Between rehearsals, the finalists spend up to two hours working with Dean Banowitz and his hairstyling team. Usually, each of the girls has a new hairstyle created especially for them.

While some of the finalists are getting their hair done, the rest can be found in the make-up room working with Mezghan Hussainy and her team of make-up artists. Both guys and girls need to wear make-up when they appear on the *American Idol* stage under the hundreds of ultra-bright lights.

When one of the girls needs longer hair to complete her look, Dean often uses clip on extensions. He also uses extensions to add color highlights, since these can be removed in seconds after the show. The extensions are made from real human hair and combine perfectly with the contestant's real hair.

Some weeks, Carrie decides to wear her hair straight. Sometimes, she goes for a curly hairstyle, which looks totally hot.

The hair and make-up teams have created some really amazing and funky looks for Nadia. She loves trying new things each week.

Even the guys look forward to working with Dean and trying out new hairstyles.

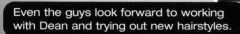

2:30 PM to 3:30 PM: Dress Rehearsal

Lights, cameras, action! Because *American Idol* is a live show, a lot can potentially go wrong. To avoid any problems, every Tuesday afternoon the contestants participate in a full dress rehearsal, complete with lights, cameras, and the *American Idol* band. For this rehearsal, they need to wear the outfit they'll be wearing for the live show, plus have their hair and make-up done.

The only differences between the dress rehearsal and the live show are that the judges don't attend the dress rehearsals and there is no studio audience. Stand-ins sit at the judges' desk.

The dress rehearsal offers each finalist their last chance to practice their song on the *American Idol* stage before having to perform it live in front of millions of people.

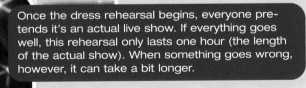

Once the dress rehearsal begins, everyone pretends it's an actual live show. If everything goes well, this rehearsal only lasts one hour (the length of the actual show). When something goes wrong, however, it can take a bit longer.

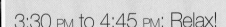

3:30 PM to 4:45 PM: Relax!

After the dress rehearsal, the finalists return to their dressing rooms to relax or touch up their hair or make-up. The countdown to show time has begun! On the set, the crew scrambles to get everything done, while the studio audience takes their seats.

5:00 PM to 6:00 PM: It's Showtime!

At exactly 5:00 PM (8:00 PM on the east coast), *American Idol* goes live. One at a time, each finalist takes center stage and offers up their performance.

After each performance, Randy, Paula, and Simon provide their critique. Sometimes, the contestants leave the stage smiling. Other times, they get backstage and burst into tears.

Every *American Idol* performance is 100 percent live. There are no second chances and no lip-syncing.

Once a Tuesday night competition show is over, the phone lines open up and the voting begins. At this point, all the finalists can do is wait until Ryan reveals the results on the following night's show. The fate of each finalist now lies in the hands of the television audience. Throughout Season 4, an average of nearly 30 million votes have been cast each week.

While you're in school or at work, hanging out with friends or watching your other favorite television shows throughout the week, all of your favorite *American Idol* finalists are busy preparing for Tuesday and Wednesday nights' shows. It's a non-stop, grueling schedule, but for the Top 12 finalists, this is a once-in-a-lifetime chance to be seen by millions of people and hopefully end the season with a record deal and a career as a recording artist. Which finalist will ultimately achieve their dreams, however, is entirely up to you!

After one of the Top 12 finalists is voted off the show on Wednesday night, the producers host a special farewell dinner in that person's honor. Affectionately called the "kiss off" dinners by the contestants and crew, these casual dinners allow the person who was voted off the show to say goodbye to their fellow contestants before packing their bags and heading home.

Only the remaining finalists, the person who was voted off the show, close family and friends, and a few producers attend these special, emotion-filled dinners.

Farewell Dinners

For Mikalah's farewell dinner, the producers picked the family-style Italian restaurant called Buca di Beppo at Universal Citywalk, which is part of the Universal Studios theme park in Hollywood.

Nadia enjoyed the restaurant's family-style dining with her mom, sisters, and a few close friends.

Nikko invited a few friends and family members to dinner.

Producer Patrick Lynn offered a toast in Mikalah's honor.

Check out Constantine's table. He was joined by his friends and family, who flew to Los Angeles to support him on the show.

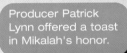

The remaining contestants, including Anthony, showed their love to Mikalah, who had befriended everyone on the show. As the youngest person on the show, Mikalah had become like everyone's younger sister.

Before dinner, the finalists spent time chatting and cheering up Mikalah and her mom, who had been on the set with Mikalah every day since the beginning of the AI season.

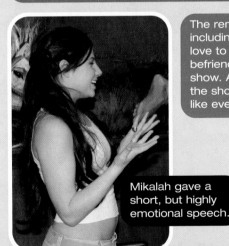

Mikalah gave a short, but highly emotional speech.

For all the remaining finalists, the farewell dinners caused mixed emotions. They feel very bad for the person leaving the show, but they're grateful they're still in the competition.

When the farewell dinners come to an end at around 11:00 PM, everyone heads home. For those still in the competition, work on the following week's show kicks off early Thursday morning.

Mikalah bid farewell to the American Idol producers and the members of the 19 Entertainment management team who attended the dinner in her honor. She thanked everyone for their love and support.

The Contestants Have Some Fun

Toward the end of the three grueling weeks that made up the semi-final round of competition, the remaining contestants needed a short break from rehearsals. They embarked on a field trip about 500 yards from CBS Television Center where *American Idol* is produced, and spent some time exploring The Grove, one of the nicest outdoor shopping malls in Southern California.

Check out these exclusive highlights from the semi-finalists' fun-filled shopping excursion.

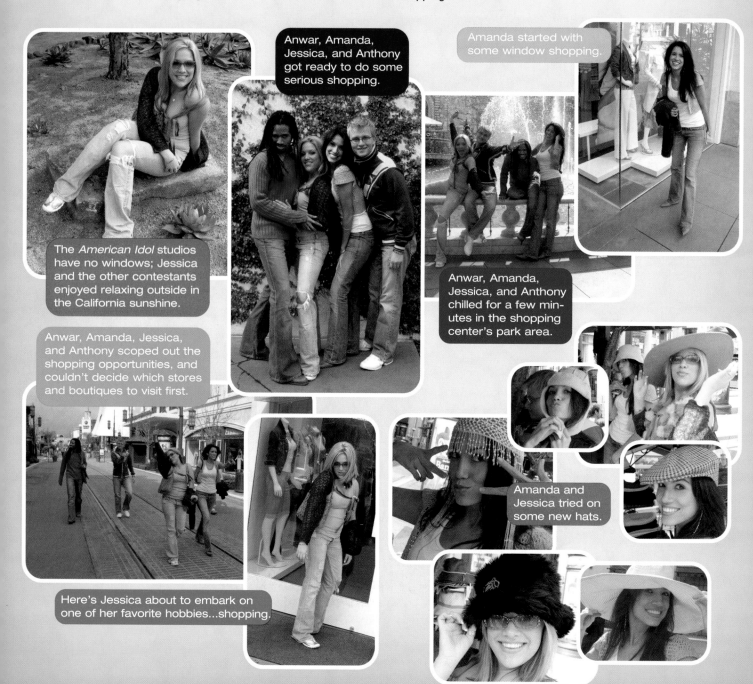

Anwar, Amanda, Jessica, and Anthony got ready to do some serious shopping.

Amanda started with some window shopping.

The *American Idol* studios have no windows; Jessica and the other contestants enjoyed relaxing outside in the California sunshine.

Anwar, Amanda, Jessica, and Anthony chilled for a few minutes in the shopping center's park area.

Anwar, Amanda, Jessica, and Anthony scoped out the shopping opportunities, and couldn't decide which stores and boutiques to visit first.

Amanda and Jessica tried on some new hats.

Here's Jessica about to embark on one of her favorite hobbies...shopping.

It's snack time!

The semi-finalists enjoyed pretzels, hot dogs, and sodas.

Amanda headed straight for the clothing racks at Abercrombie & Fitch.

Anthony bought just an ice cream cone...no ice cream. Go figure!

Jessica found a new purse.

The semi-finalists left with some new purchases.

Check out Jessica's and Mikalah's new necklaces. They picked them up at the I.D. Jewelry kiosk after discovering it's the latest trend. All the hot young celebrities are wearing jewelry from this company.

Scott found a souvenir for himself.

Scott and Janay rode the trolley that travels from one end of the outdoor shopping plaza to the other.

Janay and Scott took a break for lunch in the food court.

Scott and Janay took the "Carry Out" sign above them just a little too literally.

Travis and Mikalah shared some laughs in the park area.

While Scott chatted on the phone, Janay shopped.

Mikalah called some friends to tell them about her *American Idol* adventures.

Travis waited patiently for the girls to finish their shopping.... It was a long wait!

After a lot of walking, Mikalah's feet became tired, so she got a lift....

...then it was Mikalah's turn to try on some hats.

Travis and Mikalah explored The Grove in search of their fellow semi-finalists.

Anthony tossed a coin into the fountain and made a wish. America will know if his wish came true.

Vonzell and Bo went searching for the hottest sales.

Bo decided to give Vonzell a little push.... Of course, he was totally kidding! Nobody got wet.

Mario and Constantine shopped for sunglasses.

Hello, Jessica.... You were supposed to meet us 30 minutes ago. Where are you?

Mario enjoyed getting some fresh air as he strolled around the popular shopping plaza.

Mario tried on some hats and checked out some jewelry, too.

To avoid being recognized, Mario and Constantine tried to blend in by pretending to be statues. The ploy didn't work.

Constantine rode the trolley.

Well, all fun things must come to an end. After spending time shopping, eating, enjoying the sunshine, and exploring, it was time to get back to work. The group returned to their hectic rehearsal schedule back at the *American Idol* studios.

With record-high ratings, the most weekly votes ever cast, incredible talent, and plenty of surprises, this *American Idol* season has been amazing! There's so much more yet to come, however!

That's A Wrap!

Anthony experiences his very first rehearsal with Michael Orland and Dorian Holly. He learns that the performers use water bottles as microphones during rehearsals.

During the first days of semifinals, the Top 24 started bonding. They played cards, board games, and Twister in their dressing rooms during their free time.

The *American Idol* Season 4 compilation CD, featuring songs from each of Season 4's Top 12 finalists, has shipped to stores everywhere and offers some awesome tracks. Meanwhile, this spring, host Ryan Seacrest is releasing a line of ultra-trendy, designer T-shirts, similar to the ones that he's worn throughout the season on *American Idol*. Watch for those in stores as well!

America's favorite "metrosexual" host, who has become known for his trendy outfits and always-perfect hair, is about to release his own line of designer T-shirts. You, too, can dress as Ryan has throughout this season on *American Idol*.

When Season 4 wraps up in May 2005, the producers will soon embark on yet another journey across America to hold auditions for Season 5. Also, throughout the summer, the Top 10 finalists from Season 4—Bo Bice, Jessica Sierra, Carrie Underwood, Constantine Maroulis, Vonzell Solomon, Nadia Turner, Anthony Fedorov, Scott Savol, Anwar Robinson, and Nikko Smith—will take off on a live tour and perform in more than 50 cities. Be sure to check them out live and show them your support!

While the tour is traveling across America, the newest *American Idol* winner will release their first single in June 2005, possibly launching a chart-topping career. To learn more about the Season 5 auditions, the latest CDs, or the *American Idol* Live Tour, check out the idolonfox.com website, which is chock-full of great info!

Just because Season 4 of *American Idol* will come to an end, don't despair! Season 5 is right around the corner and will premiere in January 2006 on FOX! As Season 4 becomes a memorable part of television history, take a few moments to recall some fun moments from throughout the season!

Bo grabs a bite to eat in between rehearsals on the set.

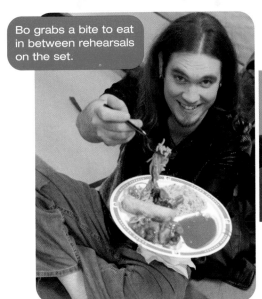

Nadia had a blast the first time she stepped foot on the *American Idol* stage to rehearse.

The Top 24 finalists were so excited to be on *American Idol*, they took photos of themselves to remember the experience.

You don't see them too much on TV, but Sharlotte Gibson, Kenya Hathaway, and Sy Smith are the three background vocalists who are always on stage performing behind band leader Rickey Minor.

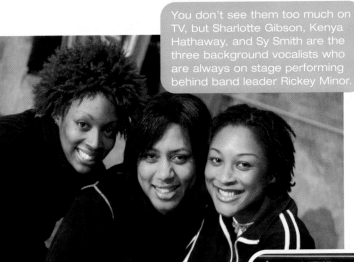

Here are the 12 guys who made it into the semi-finals. Only Bo, Constantine, Anthony, Scott, Anwar, and Nikko ultimately became Top 12 finalists.

This photo of Mario was taken just before he shocked everyone by suddenly leaving the show.

These 12 talented girls made it into the semi-finals. Only six ultimately became Top 12 finalists, however.

The brand new *American Idol* set is bigger and flashier than ever!

Are Paula and Simon having a romantic moment?

Randy Jackson showed off his musical skills when he briefly jammed with the *American Idol* band during a warm-up session.

AMANDA AVILA

For the contestants, *American Idol* is an emotional rollercoaster. Top 24 semi-finalist Melinda Lira was shocked when Ryan revealed she'd been voted off the show.

Vonzell absolutely loves Minnie Mouse!

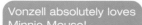

Those dreaded bleachers on stage can only mean one thing.... It's Wednesday and someone is about to be voted off the show.

Shortly after the semi-final rounds began, Bo celebrated by getting a new tattoo to commemorate the occasion.

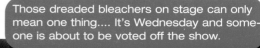

Care to guess what Ryan was thinking about when he made this face?

Anwar and Nadia checked out the *American Idol* message boards at the IdolOnFox.com Web site.

Ladies and gentleman... Nikko Smith is in the building!

Look who's having a bad hair day! It was hairstylist Dean Banowetz to the rescue!

Here's something you didn't see on TV... Constantine with straight hair! It was an experiment he didn't like. It quickly got fixed in time for the show that evening.

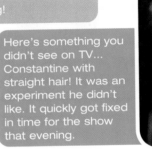

Smile Jessica, you could be the next *American Idol*!

Do the six girls in the Top 12 look hot or what? Not only are they awesome singers, they could be fashion models as well!

The Stars Love American Idol Too!

Throughout the season, a handful of celebrities dropped by the *American Idol* set to meet the finalists and see the show.

Talk show host Ricki Lake is an *American Idol* mega-fan. She came to the show with her family as a guest of Michael Orland.

Sure, she was visiting the *American Idol* set to do a story for the *Today* show, but Katie Couric admitted she's also a huge fan of the show.

Top 24 semi-finalist Jared Yates had a chance to meet La Toya London (a Top 10 finalist from Season 3) at a party in Hollywood.

The finalists were excited to meet recording artist Donny Osmond when he visited the set and signed copies of his new CD, *What I Meant To Say*, for everyone.

Camile Velasco, a Top 12 finalist from Season 3, is currently recording an album for Motown Records. She dropped by the *American Idol* set to see what it's like sitting in the audience, as opposed to performing on stage.

Ryan sat down in the Red Room for a heart-to-heart chat with *Today*'s host Katie Couric when she visited the *American Idol* set.

Michael Orland and Tony Orlando enjoyed catching up while Tony was on the set of *American Idol*.

Season 3 runner-up Diana DeGarmo enjoyed meeting Constantine Maroulis.